Sudden Selector's Guide
to Business Resources

ALCTS/CMDS SUDDEN SELECTOR'S SERIES

*Sudden Selector's Guide
to Business Resources*

SUDDEN SELECTOR'S GUIDE
to Business Resources

ROBIN BERGART

VIVIAN LEWIS

Collection Management and Development Section
of the Association for Library Collections & Technical Services
a division of the American Library Association

Chicago   2007

While extensive effort has gone into ensuring the reliability of information appearing in this book, the publisher makes no warranty, express or implied, on the accuracy or reliability of the information, and does not assume and hereby disclaims any liability to any person for any loss or damage caused by errors or omissions in this publication.

The paper used in this publication meets the minimum requirements of American National Standard for Information Sciences—Permanence of Paper for Printed Library Materials, ANSI Z39.48-1992.∞

Library of Congress Cataloging-in-Publication Data

Bergart, Robin.
    Sudden selector's guide to business resources / Robin Bergart and Vivian Lewis.
      p.   cm.—(ALCTS/CMDS sudden selector's series no. 1)
    Includes bibliographical references.
    ISBN 0-8389-8414-2
    1. Business libraries—Collection development. 2. Book selection—United States—Handbooks, manuals, etc. 3. Book selection—Canada—Handbooks, manuals, etc. I. Lewis, Vivian, 1961– II. Title.
    Z675.B8B47 2007
    025.2′18769—dc22   2006103083

ISBN-10: 0-8389-8414-2
ISBN-13: 978-0-8389-8414-7

Printed in the United States of America

11 10 09 08 07   5 4 3 2 1

EDITOR'S NOTE

This guide is part of a new Sudden Selector series from the Collection Management & Development Section of the Association for Library Collections & Technical Services division of the American Library Association. This series is designed to help library workers become acquainted with the tools, resources, individuals, and organizations that can assist in developing collections in new or unfamiliar subject areas. These guides are not intended to provide a general introduction to collection development but to quickly furnish tools for successful selection in a particular subject area.

Douglas Litts
Corcoran College of Art & Design/Gallery of Art
Series Editor

CONTENTS

FOREWORD

ROBIN BERGART AND Vivian Lewis are librarians at academic libraries in southern Ontario. Bergart started her library career as a sudden selector in charge of the business collection at the University of Guelph. With no business education or experience in business collection development, she sought out advice and expertise from more seasoned business librarians at nearby academic libraries—which is how she met Lewis.

Prior to her appointment as associate university librarian at McMaster University, Lewis held the position of business librarian at the university's Innis Library, which serves the needs of the DeGroote School of Business. Before coming to McMaster, she held several appointments in special libraries and research centers in the financial sector.

Bergart brings to this book her still-fresh experience of feeling completely at sea developing the collection of an unfamiliar discipline. Her experience is not an exceptional situation. Libraries often cannot find collection developers with corresponding subject expertise, and even when libraries can find such employees, new hires often have to take on additional subject responsibilities that may be different from those for which they were originally hired. Lewis brings a seasoned hand to the table. During her years in business, she saw and trained many sudden selectors as they moved through the ranks. In this book, she offers sage advice and many useful suggestions of resources to help develop the skills and knowledge of the sudden selector.

The authors would like to thank Bob Nardini, senior vice president and head bibliographer at YBP Library Services, who asked them to contribute to the Sudden Selector series.

The advice of the business librarians who participate in the BUSLIB-L and the Ontario Academic Business and Economics Librarians (ABEL-O) electronic discussion lists has been invaluable in writing this guide. Special thanks to Elizabeth Watson and Sophie Bury at the Peter F. Bronfman Business Library of York University, Linda Lowry at Brock University, Sandra Keys at the Dana Porter Library of the University of Waterloo, Eun-ha Spiteri at Wilfrid Laurier University, Terrence Bennett at the College of New Jersey Library, and Pat Cholach at the Hamilton Public Library for their helpful input. The authors also wish to acknowledge Pam Jacobs at Brock University for her encouragement and connecting them with Nardini in the first place.

Thank you to the authors' colleagues at the University of Guelph and McMaster University, who have been so supportive, especially Melanie Boyd, M. J. D'Elia, Doug Horne, Jeannie An, and Ines Perkovic.

INTRODUCTION AND OVERVIEW

SAMUEL JOHNSON FAMOUSLY wrote, "Knowledge is of two kinds. We know a subject ourselves, or we know where we can find information upon it." This quotation is ubiquitously cited in library literature and by librarians who believe good librarianship requires only the latter kind of knowledge. The fact is many business librarians do not come to the job with subject expertise. Most business librarians do not have an MBA, BBA, or BComm degree, much less a Ph.D. in a business field or any practical experience in business. The dearth of business librarians with relevant subject expertise is clear from the library literature. Haar writes, "job seekers with business or science training can often choose non-academic employment at salary levels that few college or university libraries can match."[1] Liu echoes, "One reason for the lack of business librarians with business degrees is the competition between the business sector and libraries, where libraries lose out. The average starting salary, including bonuses for an employee with an MBA working for a company, is way above that of a business librarian working in a public or academic library."[2]

In addition to learning something about the business discipline, new librarians must learn how collection development works, so there can be a steep learning curve to acquire the skills necessary to feel confident as a business librarian. Nevertheless, it *is* possible to become a competent business librarian without a formal business education, just as it is possible to be an art, history, or chemistry librarian by gradually learning about the information needs of the user community, building a network of colleagues, becoming familiar with the collection, and then utilizing the tools to be an effective selector.

Which are the key publishers of business books? How do you decide which company database is best for your library? Which library associations should you belong to as a business librarian? These are the kinds of questions this book will help answer. Most of what selectors learn, they learn on the job, and the authors hope that this provides some small comfort to those librarians who find themselves, perhaps even unexpectedly, plunged into the world of business. The purpose of this book is to help the sudden selector through the first few months of a new position. It is a guide to becoming a competent selector of business resources and all that this role entails: joining associations, finding mentors, monitoring electronic discussion lists, and of course, learning how to select materials for your collection.

Although the authors' experience has been mainly in academic libraries, many of the resources and selection principles included in this guide will apply to the public library setting as well. The focus of this guide is on North American business resources in English, and this guide may also be especially useful to Canadian librarians, as there is a significant lack of both business resources and guides to the literature for that market.

Please be clear about what this book is *not*. It is not a guide to the literature. There are several very good guides already available, many of which are listed in chapter 4, and you are encouraged to consult them. This book focuses on the selection phase of collection development and provides tools for becoming a better selector. It does not touch on the full process of collection development, which includes budgeting, acquisitions, deselection or weeding, preservation, and much more. Such general collection development issues as these are expertly addressed in hundreds of books and journals. For a quick introduction to collection development, the Arizona State Library, Archives, and Public Records provides a good introductory guide to collection development topics online at www.lib.az.us/cdt/ (accessed Oct. 27, 2006).

Business librarianship presents some specific challenges in addition to the usual hurdles faced by all new selectors. The sheer breadth of the discipline, and how all the various fields fit together, can be quite confusing.

Each institution will define its universe slightly differently: most libraries will include some coverage of marketing, accounting, finance, human resources, decision science, and management as core topics. However, some libraries may choose to bundle economics and business together or to add areas of specialization, such as insurance, direct selling, or real estate. There are also new and emerging areas to consider, such as e-commerce, and subjects that overlap with other disciplines, as organizational behavior does with psychology. Haythornthwaite has noted that "the problem about business information is that it can mean totally different things to different people. It is a subject without structure, there are a multiplicity of sources of variable quality and there is a total lack of co-ordination between the sources, which leads to duplication, overlap, and yawning gaps [in collections]."[3] The prudent selector is encouraged throughout this book to create and maintain clear collection policies to reduce doubt and enhance informed and consistent decision making.

It seems that almost every press publishes titles in the broad field of business. The business of business publishing is enormous, and there are business books to appeal to every interest and taste. The 2005 *Bowker Annual Library and Book Trade Almanac* reports that 5,404 business books were published in the United States in 2003.[4] The value of these publications ranges widely, so it is essential to be familiar with high-quality publishers and book series and to know which specific topics and level of treatment the library's users desire.

In addition to these challenges, there is a new language to learn—puts, calls, futures, options, beta, six sigma, and so on. You will want to have a dictionary or glossary at your side to decode unfamiliar terms and acronyms for some of the materials you are selecting. A further challenge is to sort out all the different formats and contexts in which business information is published. There are, of course, monographs, journals, and databases, but there are also business cases, working papers, and annual reports. What is available for free on the Internet, and what must be purchased? How do you decide which company database is best for your users? Can the library afford those market research reports? Business information sources tend to be complex, redundant, and expensive. To complicate matters, new technologies and formats continue to emerge. It can be overwhelming trying to assess the accuracy and reliability of competing sources.

In contrast to this seemingly enormous wealth of information is the reality that the very data a user needs may not be available. Some information is proprietary, some too expensive, and some may simply not exist. Private companies have no compunction to reveal any of their financial information. In Canada the situation is even more difficult than in the United States, given the relative dearth of business information collected by both the government and private industry. It is a challenge to convey this seemingly contradictory situation to a patron, especially when so much information seems readily available on the Internet. Market research reports pose a particularly daunting problem. These documents, so often quoted in the popular press, tend to be exceptionally costly and difficult to access. James sums up the problem:

> Unfortunately, there are few truly global research reports published and so it is often impossible to identify a suitable report to answer a global market request. Those that are available are generally very expensive . . . or they are not quite in the required sector or sub-sector. . . . Such reports are also likely to be out of date. . . . there is also the problem that the publishers and the sources are heavily orientated towards the U.K. and U.S. markets and the English language.[5]

There is no doubt that the Web has dramatically altered the face of collection development. Just getting to know the current collection is a major undertaking. In the past, collection developers could regularly browse the new journals, noting new developments in the discipline and scanning for book reviews and advertisements for new journal titles. They could easily see which reference books were most heavily used, and there were a limited number of selection tools from which to choose. When the collection was entirely in print, it was easier to grasp its scope and develop a sense of mastery over it.

Today the scene is very different. Books continue to fill the library but often are received through approval plans, so librarians are less aware of individual titles. Fewer and fewer print journals appear on the shelves, but access to electronic journals is frequently embargoed for a week to several years. Browsing an online journal is not the same as perusing a printed copy. New title announcements and reviews easily scanned in print are more scattered in the online environment. It is certainly more difficult to gain mastery of a subject in this kind of environment. Information flows in from every corner in no order of importance, making it difficult to gain an incremental understanding of the fundamentals or understand how the pieces of the discipline fit together.

In the face of all these challenges, being a subject selector can be very daunting, and you may occasionally suffer pangs of "imposter syndrome"—the sense that you are impersonating a "real" business librarian. On the other hand, the process of learning the language and literature of a discipline that is new to you can be an intellectually exciting adventure. Much like acculturating to a new language and environment, it takes time. One could even say that you have the advantage of approaching your collection responsibilities with an unbiased and open mind. The authors hope that this guide will help ease your introduction into the world of business librarianship.

HOW THIS BOOK IS ARRANGED

Chapter 1 will help you get your feet wet by giving you some guidelines of where to start as a new business selector. Once you have got the ball rolling, chapter 2 provides hints on how to keep current, stay informed, and get connected with other business librarians. Chapter 3 gets into the nuts and bolts of collection development with a list of some of the best selection tools as well as top publishers in the field of business. Online databases are probably the most expensive and difficult materials to select, and chapter 4 provides some guidance for selecting these resources.

Chapter 5 concludes this guide with some final words of wisdom by our seasoned selector, Vivian Lewis.

NOTES

1. John M. Haar, "Scholar or Librarian? How Academic Libraries' Dualistic Concept of the Bibliographer Affects Recruitment," *Collection Building* 12, no. 1–2 (1993): 18.
2. Lewis G. Liu, "The Emergence of Business Information Resources and Services on the Internet and Its Impact on Business Librarianship,"*Online Information Review* 24, no. 3 (2000): 253; Ruth A. Pagell, "Academic Business Librarians," In *Encyclopedia of Library and Information Science*, edited by M. A. Drake (New York and Basel: Dekker, 2003), 22–34.
3. Jo Haythornthwaite, ed., *Business Information Maze: An Essential Guide* (London: ASLIB, 1990), 2.
4. Dave Bogart and Julia C. Blixrud, *Bowker Annual Library and Book Trade Almanac 2005* (Medford, N.J.: Information Today, 2005).
5. Sylvia James, Compiling Global Market Research—A Tried and True Approach, *Business Information Alert* 15, no. 4 (2003): 2–3.

one

Getting Started
as a New Business Selector

As a new selector, you may have neither subject expertise, nor collection experience, so take advantage of being able to see things with "fresh" eyes. Take an investigative stance: ask lots of questions, avoid making assumptions, and find out as much as you can from your users and colleagues.

According to the late Bill Katz, professor of information studies at the State University of New York at Albany, selection is more art than science, but with practice and perseverance, the new selector can and will move "from the uncertainties of the art to the firm ground of continuing self education, experience, knowledge, and confidence. Once can become an expert. . . . To paraphrase Dr. Spock, 'You know more than you think you do.'"[1]

Selectors must remain ever-vigilant about how their own biases, interests, and backgrounds shape a collection in a particular way. To overcome these biases, selectors must read constantly, stay current with new developments in the field, and pay close attention to users' questions and needs.

GET TO KNOW YOUR USERS

Each library serves a unique population of users with different needs. Who are your core users, which information resources are they currently using, how do they prefer to access information, and what are their information needs? Do they need to develop a business plan, prepare a case study, or find data to complete a course assignment? Are your users distance-education students, international students, members of the business community, or retired persons? Find out how your library is and is not meeting users' information needs and where users go besides the library for information. That said, you will need to learn to anticipate your users' future needs as well, and you should not make collection decisions solely based on what they tell you they need *now*.

There are many ways to learn about library users and their information habits, from formal needs-assessment surveys to informal observations at the reference desk. The more methods you use, the richer the picture you can create.

Reference Questions

Take note of the questions asked at the reference desk. These will indicate users' areas of interest and their familiarity with the collection and with library use. Encourage other reference staff to let you know about the kinds of business questions posed at the desk. In an academic library, a student's question at the reference desk can prompt a follow-up discussion with that student's professor about whether the library collection is meeting course needs.

Suggestion Boxes

Libraries often have a box or bulletin board for users to ask questions and make direct requests for new material or more resources on a given subject. Carefully review submissions to learn what kinds of information users are missing.

Surveys, Focus Groups, and Interviews

Formal evaluation instruments, such as surveys and focus groups, can involve significant time and financial resources, but if done correctly, these tools can provide a rich description of users and their information needs. Personal interviews can achieve some of the same results. In an academic library, make a point of meeting with business department faculty and ask about their research interests and the courses they are teaching. Ask the faculty which kinds of resources—trade publications, academic journals, newspapers, journal indexes, and so on—are most valuable to their own research.

Course Outlines, Reading Lists, and Citation Analysis

Course syllabi and reading lists are obvious—but sometimes neglected—sources for discovering what students will need for their studies. These resources are often available on department Web sites, but if not, ask faculty to provide a print copy. While online course management systems, such as WebCT, are an extremely rich source of information, often including class notes, slides, chatrooms, and so on, these systems are typically password-protected. Analyzing the works cited in student papers and theses is incredibly time-consuming but yields rich information about collection use. Consider also attending student presentations and thesis defenses to observe which resources students are using (or not using) for their coursework.

Faculty Web Sites

Faculty Web sites are invaluable sources of information about the faculty and their publications. Regularly check department Web sites to find out about upcoming public research seminars and to see what new topics faculty and graduate students are researching. Get faculty and students engaged in collection development by encouraging them to suggest new and forthcoming titles to the library collection and key authors they think undergraduates should be reading. Be aware, however, that faculty often have narrow research interests and no one faculty member's needs should dominate the collection. You need to consider of all your users' needs—present and future.

Library Literature

Library literature is replete with data on the information-seeking skills of public and academic library users, and there are quite a few articles specifically about the information habits and needs of business collection users. These articles cannot substitute for your own local research (formal or informal), but the literature can help flag likely trends and provide a useful basis for comparison. Following are some examples from the literature:

Atkinson III, Joseph D., and Miguel Figueroa. "Information Seeking Behavior of Business Students: A Research Study." *Reference Librarian* 58, (1997): 59–73.

Dewald, Nancy H. "What Do They Tell Their Students? Business Faculty Acceptance of the Web and Library Databases for Student Research." *Journal of Academic Librarianship* 31, no. 3 (2005): 209–15.

MacEwan, Bonnie. "Understanding Users' Needs and Making Collections Choices." *Library Collections, Acquisitions, & Technical Services* 23, no. 3 (1999): 315–20.

Song, Yoo-Seong. "International Business Students: A Study on Their Use of Electronic Library Services." *Reference Services Review* 32, no. 4 (2004): 367–73.

Varga-Atkins, Tünde, and Linda Ashcroft. "Information Skills of Undergraduate Business Students—A Comparison of U.K. and International Students." *Library Management* 25, no. 1–2 (2004): 39–55.

EXPLORE AND ASSESS THE COLLECTION

Take time to explore the library's current business collection to discover its strengths and weaknesses so you can then assess collection use.

Bookshelves, Microform Cabinets, and Other Physical Collections

Walk through the stacks to get a sense of the collection's size. Observe which reference books are being used. Make it a habit to regularly check the new books shelf.

Online Resources

Explore the library's collection of online business databases to become familiar with its content and functionality. Compare searches across multiple databases. Online or telephone training from the database vendors is often available. The vendor also may be able to give you some sense of who the primary users of a database are and how they use it. Use some caution; vendors may oversell the breadth of user interest in an attempt to increase next year's commitment to their database.

Other Libraries and Bookstores and Their Web Sites

Other libraries and bookstores can help measure the comparative size, currency, and scope of your collection. Visiting other brick-and-mortar libraries (especially the reference collections) and bookstores will give you a better sense of the unique qualities of your own library's collection, or perhaps note where the collection has gaps. You can also pick up ideas about how other libraries promote and teach users about their collections.

An online analysis tool, such as the Bowker Book Analysis System (www .bowkersbookanalysis.com/bbas) will evaluate your library's collection by comparing the library catalog records against H. W. Wilson Standard Catalogs. This particular system is only useful for public library collections.

Usage Statistics

Depending on your technical infrastructure, you may be able to extract rich usage statistics for collection development purposes. Identify a call number range that covers a business area and ask technical services for a report on circulation statistics. Which titles are the most popular with your users? Similarly, request an interlibrary loan report that flags frequently requested materials. Although highly anecdotal, you can also get a sense of how your print reference collection is used by noting at the end of the day which business reference books have been pulled off the shelf. Vendors can and should provide usage data for their online databases. These data can tell you how many users have accessed the databases, whether users have been turned away because the subscription has a limited number of simultaneous users, and often, which parts of the database have been accessed.

Weeding

Weeding, or *deselection*, is an excellent opportunity not only to freshen up the collection but to get to know it intimately. Observe which collection areas are growing and which are outdated, but also be aware of which items are regularly checked out despite older publication dates. Books on business office automation from the 1970s might be discarded to free up more room for such current hot topics as leadership studies. Look for multiple copies and superseded editions that might be discarded or replaced.

Approval Plans and Collection Policies

If your library uses approval plans, read them carefully and have a representative from the vendor explain the scope and rationale behind the existing plans. Approval plans are a means of ordering books more quickly and efficiently because the plan designates which books, based on predetermined criteria, will be automatically sent to your library upon publication. These criteria include subject area, publisher, language, place of publication, audience level, and format. Your library's approval plan should be closely monitored on a regular basis to reflect changes in the user community and their information needs. The approval plan can indicate subject areas that might be missing from the collection. Approval plan vendors can also indicate which subject areas your library does not cover that other comparable institutions do cover in their approval plans.

The library's collection policy for business literature should not be neglected. It is your guide to what to include and what to exclude from the collection. If you need to do a major overhaul of the collection policy, sample policies are available in a number of library texts. Links to some policies are available from AcqWeb's Directory of Collection Development Policies on the Web (http://acqweb.library.vanderbilt.edu/cd_policy.html, **accessed date?**), although be aware that this site has not been updated since 2004. The components of public, academic, and special library collection policies are laid out in *Library Collection Development Policies: Academic, Public, and Special Libraries.*[2]

REFRESH YOUR COLLECTION DEVELOPMENT KNOWLEDGE

Dozens of books and articles are published on collection development every year. Use this literature as the need arises. You can find many general works that cover collection development from A to Z as well as literature devoted to specific questions on weeding, gifts, collection evaluation, approval plans, and so on. You can also learn a lot by asking questions of senior library staff, vendors, and colleagues. Some libraries provide manuals to orient new selectors to the process of collection development. If your library does not have such a manual, write one yourself while everything is still fresh and the next new hire will benefit from your experience.

Peggy Johnson's *Fundamentals of Collection Development and Management* (American Library Association, 2004) is a highly readable overview of collection development theory and practice. The work includes a glossary, excellent recommended reading lists, and an appendix of selection aids. One review asserts that it "will stand for years as a standard text for students of library and information management, and as a *vade mecum* for busy professionals."[3]

Another older but still relevant and readable book is the *Guide for Training Collection Development Librarians* (American Library Association, 1996), edited by Susan L. Fales. Fales echoes the sentiment expressed earlier in this chapter that "a selector's primary responsibility is to identify and build a coherent body of knowledge on a given subject *which meets the information needs of the library's primary clients, who are identified in the collection development policies*" [emphasis added].[4]

AcqWeb (http://acqweb.library.vanderbilt.edu/acqweb, accessed Oct. 27, 2006) is a great Web site for all collection-related matters, with links to bibliographic verification tools, collection policies, and collection-development issues from preservation to gifts to usage statistics.

The Association for Library Collections & Technical Services (ALCTS), a division of the American Library Association (ALA), offers workshops and Web courses on basic collection development (www.ala.org/ala/alcts/alcts conted/alctsceevents/events.htm, Oct. 27, 2006).

TEACH OTHERS

Most libraries have mechanisms for keeping staff up to date on new resources. Seek out such opportunities with enthusiasm. In the process of teaching other staff about the business collection, you will gain much greater understanding of the subject area and of the resources yourself.[5] A Georgetown University business librarian provides an online guide to using complex business databases at www.library.georgetown.edu/bic/help.htm (accessed Oct. 27, 2006), which you may want to refer to when preparing to teach colleagues how to use the business databases.

NOTES

1. Bill Katz, "Book Selection and Collection Building: Comments on the Art" In *Recruiting, Educating, and Training Librarians for Collection Development*, edited by Peggy Johnson and Shelia S. Intner (Westport, Conn.: Greenwood, 1994), 5.
2. For example, Frank W. Hoffmann, and Richard J. Wood, *Library Collection Development Policies: Academic, Public, and Special Libraries* (Lanham, MD: Scarecrow, 2005).
3. G. E. Gorman, review in *Library Collections, Acquisitions, and Technical Services* 28, no. 4 (Winter 2004): 489
4. Susan L. Fales, ed., *Guide for Training Collection Development Librarians* (Chicago: American Library Association, 1996), 10.
5. James Cory Tucker, "Getting Down to Business: Library Staff Training," *Reference Services Review* 32, no. 3 (2004): 293–301.

two

Getting up to Speed
Strategies for Current Awareness

Keeping up with new publications, databases, Web sites, technologies, and research developments can be daunting and requires a significant commitment to staying informed and in the loop. Business librarians connect in many different online communities and in person at courses and conferences. Find the communities that match your particular needs and take advantage of a supportive network of people happy to offer advice and encouragement.

Because it is impossible to be aware of, much less manage, every available current awareness tool, try new tools out but discard them if you do not find them incredibly useful. If you find a particular newsletter or electronic discussion list is draining your time more than it is helping you, drop it.

This chapter suggests the following resources to tap into established networks of business librarians and other resources to deepen your subject expertise and, perhaps more importantly, to strengthen your knowledge of how to *find* business information:

- current awareness newsletters;
- electronic discussion lists;

of the Public Forum Institute, a U.S. organization to advance public discourse. This weekly newsletter is a digest of news and information on "various trends driving the [American] innovation economy"—in other words, articles of interest for entrepreneurs and other business professionals.

ResourceShelf Newsletter
www.resourceshelf.com

This popular current awareness newsletter, compiled and edited by Washington-based librarian Gary Price, covers more than business resources, but it is well worth browsing. The ResourceShelf Web site links to a database titled the List of Lists (www.specialissues.com/lol), created by Gary Price and maintained by Trip Wyckoff of Specialissues.com. This is a great resource for quick reference of the top-performing banks, top dairy cooperatives, fastest-growing consumer goods companies, and so on.

SLA Connections
www.sla.org/content/Shop/enewsletters/slacommunicate
index.cfm

The Special Libraries Association's monthly newsletter, SLA Connections, includes news snippets, reviews, notices of upcoming conferences, and events.

VIP
www.vivavip.com/vip

This monthly review of business information products and previews of new products is available by subscription.

ELECTRONIC DISCUSSION LISTS

Join an electronic discussion list, and you join a virtual community. The following lists are all moderately to very active. Consider them virtual fora for your questions. Subscription information can be found on the Web sites provided.

ACQNET-L
www.infomotions.com/serials/acqnet

Acquisitions librarians meet on this list, and while not all topics posted on ACQUNET-L will be of interest to the collections librarian, expect to see relevant job postings, alerts of upcoming events and conferences, and general news to keep you in the loop of collection and acquisitions issues.

BUSINFOTEACHERS
http://listserv.kent.edu/archives/businfoteachers.html

BUSINFOTEACHERS serves librarians who teach business or business information.

BUSLIB-L
http://listserv.boisestate.edu/archives/buslib-1.html

BUSLIB-L is where the action is when it comes to business librarianship. Contributors ask questions, evaluate business resources, and keep one another informed on developments in the world of business librarianship. Often new selectors post queries about how to get up to speed on particular subject areas of their selection responsibilities.

COLLDV-L
http://infomotions.com/serials/colldv-l

COLLDV-L is the moderated discussion list of ALCTS.

HOSPITALITY-LIB

This niche discussion list for hospitality and tourism librarians has a small membership.

To subscribe, send an e-mail to listserv@listserv.cc.ucf.edu with the command: subscribe hospitality-lib.

SLABF-L

The Business and Finance Division of the Special Libraries Association hosts this list, which in addition to discussing business issues, posts announcements, calls for nominations, and conference planning information.

To subscribe, send an e-mail to listserv@lists.psu.edu with the command: subscribe SLABF-L. Archives are posted at http://lists.psu.edu/cgi -bin/wa?A0=SLABF-L.

Strategis Headlines
http://strategis.ic.gc.ca/epic/internet/inwn-qn.nsf/en/h_wn00152e.html

Strategis is Industry Canada's portal to business and consumer information. This is a complex site, so the weekly e-mail update keeps users abreast of new information.

BLOGS

The number of library-related blogs created by organizations and individual librarians grows daily. You can use such blog search engines as Technorati (www.technorati.com) to find more library blogs. Blogs are not only places to find out what others are thinking about or reading but places to find a virtual community.

Library Collections and Acquisitions
http://libcollections.blogspot.com

The Library Collections and Acquisitions blog focuses on collections and acquisition issues in Canadian libraries.

Library Juice
http://libraryjuicepress.com/blog

Library Juice was originally an e-zine written and compiled by librarian and activist Rory Litwin. The blog's

> "concerns are with information as a public good; privacy; corporate and government censorship and disinformation; information policy; the meaning of literacy in the electronic age; the information society; intellectual freedom; the decline of the public sphere; deprofessionalization and other work issues for librarians; information ethics; and the decline of civilization and the meaning of that decline for the library profession."

Library Stuff
www.librarystuff.net

As the name suggests, this blog covers a lot of ground, but it is useful for general current awareness about libraries and technology, new resources, and politics.

Ohio University Business Blog
www.library.ohiou.edu/subjects/businessblog

Business and economics librarian Chad F. Boeninger keeps students and faculty up to date at Ohio University with this blog, which includes information relevant to selection.

ONLINE Insider
www.onlineinsider.net

Marydee Ojala, editor of *ONLINE* magazine, maintains this blog that provides information and reviews about electronic information products.

The Shifted Librarian

www.theshiftedlibrarian.com

The Shifted Librarian blog provides up-to-date information on advances in information technology.

SEARCH ENGINES AND PORTALS FOR BUSINESS INFORMATION

The following search engines and portals sometimes point to sites that generic search engines like Google miss:

Best of the Web Business Web Sites

www.ala.org/ala/rusa/rusaourassoc/rusasections/brass/ brassprotools/bestofthebestbus/bestbestbusiness.htm

Members of the ALA's Reference and User Service Association's Business Reference and Services Section compile this small, handpicked selection of Web sites.

BUBL Link

http://bubl.ac.uk

BUBL Information Service at the University of Strathclyde in Glasgow selects and categorizes academic Internet resources using the Dewey Decimal Classification System. For *highly* selected lists of business resources, drill down to sections 381 and 382.

Business 2.0 Web Guide

http://money.cnn.com/magazines/business2

This directory of selected Web sites covers marketing, career, business, and management information.

Business.com

www.business.com/

Business.com is a business search engine and directory.

CEOExpress

www.ceoexpress.com/default.asp

The CEOExpress portal links to business news and magazines, business schools, and a variety of general reference Web sites.

INFOMINE

http://infomine.ucr.edu

INFOMINE is a virtual library of Web sites relevant to academics and university students.

Internet Public Library

www.ipl.org

The school of information and library studies at the University of Michigan created this site in 1995 as a hierarchical database of *prescreened*, annotated Web sites. There is quite a good selection of business sites on such topics as accounting, banking, e-commerce, and real estate. The site also features some specialized pathfinders based on requests at public libraries, such as finding resources for starting a small business or job hunting.

Librarian's Internet Index

http://lii.org

Maintained primarily by California State Library system and Washington State Library staff, the Librarian's Internet Index provides prescreened, annotated Web sites. There are few business sites, save the eighty-six sites on business in California, so business collection developers will not be overwhelmed.

QuickMBA

www.quickmba.com

This quick reference guide covers key topics students encounter in MBA programs.

RePEc

http://repec.org

Although RePEc, an abbreviation of Research Papers in Economics, is an economics database, it is included here because it is widely used by business researchers with an interest in economics. The database project provides links to thousands of journal articles, working papers, and author contacts. Also of note for economics research are the Resources for Economists on the Internet Web site at www.rfe.org and the agricultural and applied economics site AgEcon Search at http://agecon.lib.umn.edu.

Research Tools and Papers

www.virtualpet.com/rtools.htm

Maintained by Polson Enterprises, a new product development firm, this site provides links to information on how to perform industry, patent, and market research; how to evaluate company Web sites; and more.

Search Systems.net

www.searchsystems.net

Search Systems searches U.S. public records.

SMEALSearch

http://smealsearch2.psu.edu/index.html

Named for the business school at Pennsylvania State University, SMEAL searches academic business literature on the Web.

Yahoo! Finance

http://finance.yahoo.com

This well-known and popular site provides links to business news, stock markets, and a variety of other business information.

LIBRARY ASSOCIATIONS AND CONFERENCES

The value of becoming actively involved in associations cannot be overstated. As a member you become part of a network of professionals with expertise, ideas, and enthusiasm to share. National associations have regional divisions and local chapters so there is an opportunity to connect with a smaller (and geographically closer) group of people. Many associations publish useful newsletters and provide online resources and reviews to help in collection development. Conferences afford the opportunity to visit vendor exhibits, attend educational sessions, and exchange information with colleagues.

Business and Finance (BF) Division of the Special Libraries Association (SLA)

www.slabf.org

BF publishes a quarterly *BF Bulletin* of reviews and helpful articles on the "business" of being a business librarian. It also publishes a bibliography of publications by BF members. BF members benefit from the mentorship and professional development opportunities open to all SLA members. SLA's annual conference, which takes place in June, offers many sessions relevant to business librarians.

Business Reference and Services Section (BRASS)

www.ala.org/ala/rusa/rusaourassoc/rusasections/brass/brass.htm

BRASS is an interest group of the Reference and User Services Association (RUSA), a division of ALA. The BRASS Web site posts past conference presentations and handouts, guides to the literature, a list of core resources guidelines for U.S. academic librarians preparing reports for the Association to Advance Collegiate Schools of Business, and best business Web sites. BRASS offers sessions at the ALA Annual Conference and meets at ALA's Midwinter Meeting.

Canadian Association of Special Libraries and Information Services (CASLIS)
www.cla.ca/caslis/index.htm

CASLIS, a division of the Canadian Library Association (CLA), hosts local events across Canada.

Canadian Library Association
www.cla.ca

Canada's national association hosts an annual conference and offers networking and education opportunities. Two of CLA's interest groups, Business Information (www.cla.ca/about/igroups/business.htm) and Collection Development and Management (www.cla.ca/about/igroups/collection.htm), are useful for business selectors.

Charleston Conference
www.katina.info/conference

Publishers, vendors, and librarians meet in Charleston, South Carolina, to discuss collections issues of mutual interest at this annual gathering.

Collection Development and Evaluation Section (CODES)
www.ala.org/ala/rusa/rusaourassoc/rusasections/codes/codes.htm

CODES is a section of RUSA. It is devoted to collection development interests in all types of libraries.

Collection Management and Development Section (CMDS)
www.ala.org/ALCTS

CMDS is a section of ALCTS division. ALCTS hosts programs and events at the ALA Annual Conference and provides other continuing education opportunities and resources to members. CMDS engages in several committees and discussion and interest groups for academic and public librarians. CMDS also initiates publications and coordinates educational opportunities in the area of collection development. Click on the "Collections" tab of the ALCTS Web site to navigate to the CMDS section.

Public Library Association (PLA)
www.pla.org/ala/pla/pla.htm

PLA is a division of ALA and serves those who work in public libraries. PLA publishes *Public Libraries* and holds a biennial conference.

MENTORSHIP AND NETWORKING

Sudden selectors can benefit from seeking out other business selectors working in nearby libraries. Academic Business and Economic Librarians in Ontario (ABEL-O) is an example of an informal network of business and economics selectors who share information over an e-mail list and meet occasionally to discuss issues of common interest. The more veteran selectors are a great boon to the new selectors, and new selectors bring their own unique knowledge and talents to the group. The formal term for this kind of network is a *community of practice*, where members of the community gain a sense of belonging, identity, and terrific learning opportunities.[1]

Mentorship can be an informal relationship with a more senior colleague or a formal program with scheduled meetings and a plan to meet certain objectives. In 1999, the Association of Research Libraries reported twenty-one academic libraries offering formal mentoring programs.[2] More and more library associations and their local chapters, as well as library and information schools, are offering mentorship opportunities. Mentorship is a mutually beneficial relationship, so don't feel shy approaching a respected senior colleague about the possibility of creating a mentoring relationship.

Following are two examples of mentoring programs available from associations:

RUSA/CODES New Member Mentoring Program
www.ala.org/ala/rusa/rusaourassoc/rusasections/codes/
codesprotools/mentorprogram/mentorprogram.htm

The CODES section of RUSA offers a New Member Mentoring Program to help new members and those new to the profession.

SLA Virtual Advisors
www.sla.org/content/jobs/advisor.cfm

SLA's Virtual Advisors program offers online access to mentors 24/7 and links to local mentorship programs through SLA divisions and chapters. SLA has developed a *Mentorship Handbook* available for download and offers virtual seminars on career development.

CONTINUING EDUCATION

Your local business school may offer nondegree continuing education or professional development courses. If your library is on the campus of your local business school, this may also be a good opportunity to get to know the faculty and curriculum. You may be able to audit a credit course and learn about business, while also observing the business students who use your library. Community colleges, business development organizations, and city-run continuing education programs often offer basic business courses. Many library schools offer weekend and online courses for practitioners to gain new skills and refresh their knowledge. If there are no continuing education courses offered in your area, consider some of the following possibilities:

ALA Continuing Education Clearinghouse
www.ala.org

Search for the Continuing Education Clearinghouse page on the ALA Web site for a database of all ALA workshops, conferences, and online learning opportunities.

American Management Association
www.amanet.org/elearn/index.htm

The American Management Association offers a variety of online business skills courses.

Canadian Securities Course
www.csi.ca

The Canadian Securities Institute provides courses and certification to employees of the financial industry. These courses are recognized by the Canadian Securities Commission and the Investment Dealers Association in Canada. The institute offers several different courses and seminars, including the basic Canadian Securities Course, which is an overview of the Canadian economy and introduction to financial markets, regulation of the industry, and investment products that even a beginner can understand.

The Education Institute
www.thepartnership.ca/cgi-bin/site/showPage.cgi?page=education/index.html

A partnership of eight Canadian provincial library associations, the Education Institute offers online courses and teleconferences on a variety of topics, including an online course titled Business Web Resources for Non-business Specialists.

Society of Competitive Intelligence Professionals
www.scip.org

The Society of Competitive Intelligence Professionals offers online courses, workshops, and conferences on the gathering and assessment of business information.

SLA Professional Development Center
www.sla.org/content/learn/index.cfm

SLA runs continuing education courses as part of its annual conference. SLA also offers a virtual learning series on topics for professional advancement and Click University, an online learning community where members can take short courses and even earn certificates and library science degrees from Drexel University and Syracuse University.

Kovacs Consulting
www.kovacs.com/training.html

Diane Kovacs is an information consultant who offers online courses on competitive intelligence and small business research on the Web.

REGULAR READING

Staying on top of current business news can go a long way toward developing confidence, learning business vocabulary, and understanding business world issues. In addition to the business section of your daily paper, browse some of the following publications. Many of them offer free current awareness e-mail alerts or Really Simple Syndication (RSS) news feeds. Most of these publications run book reviews, so you can stay current *and* do collection development at the same time.

Business

Business 2.0

Canadian Business

CNN/Money

Economist

Financial Times or FT.com

Forbes

Fortune

Harvard Business Review

Ivey Business Journal

Sloan Management Review

Wall Street Journal

Collection development

Against the Grain

Chronicle of Higher Education

Collection Building

College & Research Libraries (ALA)

Information Advisor

Information Today (SLA)

Journal of Academic Librarianship

Journal of Business and Finance Librarianship

NetConnect

ONLINE

Reference Librarian

Reference Services Review

Research Strategies

Searcher

Wired

NOTES

1. ABEL-O member Linda Lowry of Brock University, a researcher of communities of practice, presented a session titled "Communities of Practice for Subject Librarians: Making Connections across the Profession to Enhance Interaction and Knowledge Sharing" at the Ontario Library Association's 2006 Super Conference, Toronto, Feb. 3, 2006. For more information on communities of practice, see the following books cited in her presentation: Etienne Wenger, *Communities of Practice* (London: Oxford, 1998); Etienne Wenger, Richard McDermott, and William M. Snyder, *Cultivating Communities of Practice: A Guide to Managing Knowledge* (Boston: Harvard Bus. Sch., 2002). Lowry's full bibliography is available at http://www.accessola2.com/superconference2006/fri/1005/bib.doc (Oct. 27, 2006).

2. Wittkopf, Barbara J. *SPEC Kit 239 Mentoring Programs in ARL Libraries* (Washington, D.C.: Association of Research Libraries, 1999).

three

Selection Tools

BUSINESS INFORMATION IS published and presented in many different formats. A good business collection includes a balanced mix of formats selected on the basis of local needs. The mix typically includes some combination of monographs and electronic books, trade publications, business magazines and scholarly journals, business cases, market research reports and industry surveys, business legislation and government data, audiovisual material, country information, company financials, and annual reports. Reference collections, whether online or in print, typically include company, trade, and employment directories; biographical and lexical dictionaries; almanacs, handbooks, encyclopedias, industry and occupational code books; loose-leaf reporters; and market share data. Academic libraries often add working papers and conference proceedings. Public libraries sometimes include a local business vertical file.

The prudent selector should be aware of two key facts: First, the precise components of the mix will change with time. New technologies, such as blogs, wikis, podcasts, open access sources, and so on, are becoming mainstream. Second, most users are more content-driven than format-driven. As a recent OCLC study concluded, information seekers are "'form agnostic' in that they do not care much what sort of container—such as a book, journal, blog or a Web page—the content comes from."[1]

Many of these information sources are now available electronically as part of online business databases, which will be discussed further in chapter 5. This chapter provides places to find business information in all of its formats, with a particular emphasis on monographs. Books are still the building blocks of library collections and the most logical place for new selectors to focus their energies while learning to navigate the business literature.

The selection process for books is aided in many libraries by library approval plans—book profiles created in collaboration with vendors so that the library automatically receives certain books. Approval plans match books against carefully determined subjects and a variety of *nonsubject parameters*, such as audience level, price, language, place of publication, and so on. If a book meets all these criteria, the library receives a copy. Major approval plan vendors provide additional selection guidance by providing noteworthy, bestseller, and book award titles and reports of selections made by peer libraries and major research collections, such as recent acquisitions of the Baker Library of the Harvard Business School (www.library.hbs.edu/bakerbooks/recent/). However, approval plans are just one kind of selection tool, and these plans are not a panacea for the selector, as they must be continuously monitored to ensure that they are meeting the exigencies of the library's collection policies. This chapter provides some other selection tools that will help you build your business collection, including:

- subject guides and collections at other libraries;
- reviews, bestseller lists, and verification tools;
- guides to the literature;
- review articles;
- core journals; and
- publisher catalogs and Web sites.

SUBJECT GUIDES AND COLLECTIONS AT OTHER LIBRARIES

Subject guides are created for library users, but these guides are useful to new selectors because they highlight core resources in a particular subject and are freely available on library Web sites. Search library home pages for *subject guides, pathfinders,* or *resource guides.* The best subject guides not only list but also annotate and evaluate resources. Some libraries also list new or most-popular books on the library Web site, which can be very useful. The following is only a small sample of some good business subject guides:

Business Books: Core Collections and Much More
www.uflib.ufl.edu/businesslibrary/books/books.htm

University of Florida librarian Peter Z. McKay keeps a list of essential books for every imaginable area of business and economics. Full bibliographic information is provided, including book price; an archive of books acquired since 2002 is also available.

Library of Congress Business Reference Services
www.loc.gov/rr/business

This site provides rich access to Web sites, books, and data on anything and everything remotely related to business and industry. Beyond the basic categories of accounting, international business, and so on, there are links to resources on much more specific and esoteric topics, such as the pyrotechnic industry, history of the New York Stock Exchange, and wedding industry research. A number of Canadian sources are listed as well.

Core Competencies for Business Reference
www.ala.org/ala/rusa/rusaourassoc/rusasections/brass/
brassprotools/corecompetencies/corecompetenciesbusiness.htm

Produced by the BRASS Education Committee of RUSA, this site — which is part subject guide, part FAQ, and part definitions of common terms — is intended "to serve as a basic subject guide for answering business questions in a general reference setting in small- to medium-sized libraries." The site covers accounting, advertising and marketing, banking, company and industry research, insurance, international business, investment and finance, jobs and human resources, small business, and taxation.

Harvard Business School Baker Library Research Guides
www.library.hbs.edu/guides

These concise research guides point to essential sources covering a wide range of business topics, from advertising to venture capital, with biotechnology, globalization, and motion pictures in between.

College in Research Library News "Internet Reviews"
www.ala.org/ala/acrl/acrlpubs/crlnews/collegeresearch.htm

The "Internet Reviews" column in *College & Research Library News* highlights the best Internet sites on a given topic, some of which are relevant for business research.

Library and Archives Canada New Books Service
www.collectionscanada.ca/newbooks/index-e.html

New and forthcoming Canadian electronic and print publications are listed on this Web site. Updated monthly, the site allows users to search for titles or browse topics organized by Dewey Decimal Classification. To browse for business titles, look under 380: Commerce, Communication, Transportation.

New York Public Library's Science, Industry, and Business Library Guides
www.nypl.org/research/sibl/guides

As the name suggests, these research guides are a mix of science, industry, and business. Business selectors might serendipitously find something of interest that they would not find on a Web site devoted only to business, such as climate data; tsunami resources; and apparel, fashion, and textiles sources.

Toronto Public Library's Virtual Reference Library
http://vrl.torontopubliclibrary.ca

Click on Business, Finance, and Economics section of this site for Canadian and international sources of free online business information. Canadian sites are marked with a little Canadian flag.

REVIEWS, BESTSELLER LISTS, AND VERIFICATION TOOLS

Most library and business publications include reviews of business books and other business resources. Verification tools are book catalogs, online booksellers, and other databases that provide bibliographic information.

Amazon.com
www.amazon.com or www.amazon.ca

Use this commercial Web site to find quick book reviews (albeit mostly by nonexperts), track down bestsellers, and verify bibliographic information.

Bowker's BooksInPrint.com Professional and Global BookInPrint.com
www.bowker.com/products/online.htm

BooksInPrint.com, with more than 5 million book records, and Global BooksinPrint, with 13 million are subscription-only databases. Both have records on publishers, book agents, distributors, and book reviews. Title records provide abstracts, prices, availability, audience level, and reviews

BooksInPrint.com divides business and economics titles into more than 140 discrete searchable subject areas.

Booklist
www.booklistonline.com

Booklist is the ALA's print publication of book reviews for school and public librarians, and it publishes a top-ten business books list. *Booklist* Online is a Web site that provides some free *Booklist* content and a subscription-only database of archived reviews and features.

Books for Business
www.booksforbusiness.com

Former librarian Jane Cooney owns Books for Business, a Toronto bookstore specializing in business literature. Users can subscribe to the B4B Bestseller Mailing List to see what real-life business people are reading.

BusinessWeek
www.businessweek.com

BusinessWeek magazine publishes a bestseller list of popular business titles.

CHOICE: Current Reviews for Academic Librarians
www.ala.org/ala/acrl/acrlpubs/choice/home.htm

CHOICE, a print and online publication of ALA, has been a standard collection tool for decades. The reviews and recommendations of monographs and Web sites in *CHOICE* are particularly helpful in making purchase decisions if your collection budget is tight.

Information Advisor
www.informationadvisor.com

Published monthly, this newsletter frequently reviews the features of databases to aid in selection.

Information Outlook
www.sla.org/content/Shop/Information/index.cfm

This monthly magazine of SLA features a column, Web Sites Worth a Click, that often covers topics of interest to business librarians.

Library Journal
www.libraryjournal.com

Library Journal is a well-known library publication issued twenty times per year. The corresponding online site features a collection development page with most-borrowed lists from public libraries, readers' advisory, and collection building tools.

Library of Congress

http://catalog.loc.gov/webvoy.htm

The Library of Congress online catalog is a good tool for quick verification of bibliographic information. It also provides links to other public, academic, and research libraries around the world.

New York Times Book Review

Most newspapers have a book review section, and some feature business books in their business sections. Other popular sources for current book reviews are *TLS Weekly, Globe and Mail, Economist, New York Review of Books, Atlantic Monthly, Wall Street Journal,* and *Time.*

OCLC WorldCat

www.oclc.org/firstsearch/content/worldcat

WorldCat brings together records from more than 50,000 libraries worldwide. Use this FirstSearch database to verify citations and to find out how many libraries own a particular item.

Publishers Weekly

www.publishersweekly.com

Publishers Weekly lists forthcoming titles on all subject areas and lists upcoming author tours.

VIP

www.vivavip.com

VIP is a subscription-based monthly newsletter that reviews and compares business information products.

Video Librarian

www.videolibrarian.com

As the name suggests, this bimonthly print publication reviews videos. A subscription includes access to a searchable online database.

Although some of the resources in these following guides are out of date, these are still very useful books to keep handy, as they are usually annotated, and include glossaries and explanations of how business literature is organized. In doing so, these resources truly guide you through the literature rather than simply listing sources.

Berkman, Robert I. *The Skeptical Business Searcher: The Information Advisor's Guide to Evaluating Web Data, Sites, and Sources.* Medford, N.J.: Information Today, 2004.

Business researchers can and do use the free Web resources for much of their research. Berkman's book is a good refresher on how to maintain a critical eye while searching the Web and a reminder of when *not* to use the Web. The book contains helpful strategies for making the most of Web research as well as appendices with prescreened, recommended Web sites. This book and the others in the CyberAge Books series have an accompanying Web page (http://books.infotoday.com/books) that hosts an updated list of links mentioned in the book.

Bibliographic Guide to Business and Economics. 3 vols. (Boston: G. K. Hall)

The business and economics publications cataloged by the Library of Congress (Library of Congress classifications HA-HJ) and the New York Public Library during the past year are reflected in this three-volume annual.

Business: The Ultimate Resource. Cambridge, Mass.: Perseus, 2002.

This 2,172 page tome is a Swiss Army–knife of a book that includes an encyclopedia of business concepts, strategies, and people, a dictionary of business terms, a country almanac and, for collection purposes, both a list of the most influential business books of all time, and a selection of sources arranged by topic.

Butler, F. Patrick *Business Research Sources: A Reference Navigator.* Boston: McGraw-Hill, 1999.

The author, a professor of international business, may be a librarian at heart because he introduces his book with the much-loved Samuel Johnson quotation cited at the beginning of this book. This is a highly selective guide to approximately 100 business sources. Although some of the information is now out of date, much is still valid, and even the out of date information makes for interesting historical reading. For example, he describes Wilson's Business Periodicals Index (now online) as "these homely blue-covered indexes" (158). Butler's explanations transcend the usual *what* and *how* of other guides and explore why the sources he has selected are so important to business researchers.

Coman Jr., Edwin T. "Business literature." In *Encyclopedia of Library and Information Science,* edited by Miriam A. Drake. New York and Basel: Dekker, 2003.

Coman presents a short history of business literature from the Babylonians to twentieth-century scientific management, followed by a select list of key works in specific fields of business.

Cooper, Donald R., and Pamela S. Schindler. *Business Research Methods*, 9th ed. Boston: McGraw Hill, 2006.

Although undergraduate business students are the primary audience for this introductory approach to research design, data collection and analysis, and secondary business resources, it is highly readable and useful for the business librarian as well.

Crainer, Stuart *The Ultimate Business Library: The Greatest Books That Made Management*, 3d. ed. Oxford: Capstone, 2003.

From Sun Tzu to Peter Drucker, the author has chosen what they believe are the most influential management books of all time.

Diamond, Wendy, and Michael R. Oppenheim. *Marketing Information: A Strategic Guide for Business and Finance Libraries*. Binghamton, N.Y.: Haworth, 2004.

This is a terrific handbook to key sources in marketing in the broadest sense. It includes chapters on advertising, demographics, country information, and e-commerce. Key resources are interspersed with tips on using and understanding the sources. The work includes a handy checklist of major sources for every aspect of marketing—from ad copy to trade shows.

Foster, Pamela *Online Business Sourcebook*, 2nd ed. München: K.G. Saur, 2002.

Foster's guide to electronic business databases (Web-based and CD-ROM) describes more databases than any one public or academic library would ever own, but it is a good overview of the products that are available.

Dillon, Martin, and Sheila Graff Hysell, eds. *ARBA In-depth : Economics and Business*. Westport, Conn. and London: Libraries Unlimited, 2004.

American Reference Books Annual (ARBA) is a standard reference tool that well-known to most librarians. This is the first and only edition devoted to economics and business. It is useful for academic, public, and special libraries with good reviews and bibliographic information of print reference sources (directories, encyclopedias, almanacs, and so on) published between 1996 and 2003. The reviews include a description of the reference book and how it is organized and recommends it for particular audiences (for example, high school students, undergraduate accounting students, and so on). Topics covered are general works, accounting, business education, investment and consumer guides, finance and banking, industry and manufacturing, insurance, international business, labor, management, marketing and trade, occupational health and safety, office practices, real estate, and taxation.

Karp, Rashelle S., and Bernard S. Schlessinger, eds. *The Basic Business Library: Core Resources*, 4th ed. Westport, Conn.: Greenwood, 2002.

Part 1 of this title is a list of core print reference tools for business. Each entry includes notes on authority, scope, and an evaluation. Part 2 is selection of essays on business librarianship and guides to major online databases, U.S. government and investment sources, and business periodicals.

Klopper, Susan M., ed. *Introduction to Online Accounting and Financial Research Series*. Mason, Ohio: Thomson/Texere, 2004.

As with the other books in the Business Research Series, this book advises the reader on doing online research for a particular business need, whether it is intellectual property, competitive intelligence, accounting, legal, investment, company research, or in this case, accounting and financial research.

Jackson, Robert M. *The Entrepreneur's Reference Guide to Small Business Information*, 3d ed. Library of Congress Business Reference Services Web site, www.loc.gov/rr/business/guide/guide2 (accessed Jan. 5, 2006).

Originally created by the Business Enrichment Advisory Team at the Library of Congress, this third edition of the guide cites reference books and how-to books on entrepreneurship.

Lang, Eva M., and Jan Davis Tudor. *Best Web Sites for Financial Professionals, Business Appraisers, and Accountants*, 2nd ed. Hoboken, N.J.: Wiley, 2003.

As the title suggests, this book lists Web sites for business information, specifically, sites for finding information on private and public companies, market and industry research, intellectual property, executive compensation, taxes and accounting, and international business information.

Lanza, Sheri R. *International Business Information on the Web: Searcher Magazine's Guide to Sites and Strategies for Global Business Research*. Medford, N.J: Information Today, 2001.

The Web sites listed in this book are chambers of commerce, stock exchanges, and other business sites around the world. The book is organized geographically and truly does have a global scope, with some search strategy tips interspersed throughout.

Lavin, Michael R. *Business Information: How to Find It, How to Use It*, 3d ed. Phoenix, Ariz.: Oryx , 2002.

This book describes business concepts from the novice's perspective. Various sources are compared on their presentation of business information.

Moss, Rita W., and Diane W. Strauss. *Strauss's Handbook of Business Information: A Guide for Librarians, Students, and Researchers*, 2nd ed. Westport, Conn.: Libraries Unlimited, 2004.

Moss and Strauss's classic is highly recommended for all business librarians. It is a diamond mine of information that includes not only annotated sources but explanations of how to read and use business information. The first part of the book examines how business information is organized and the key formats in which it is found (directories, periodicals, online databases, and so on). The second part of the book is a very useful introduction to the major fields of business, explaining key concepts and sources for information in each field (marketing, accounting and taxation, money, credit and banking, stocks, bonds, mutual funds, futures and options, insurance, and real estate). There are several appendixes on acronyms, key economic indicators, Web sites, and more.

Pagell, Ruth A., and Michael Halperin. *International Business Information : How to Find It, How to Use It*, 2nd ed. Phoenix, Ariz.: Oryx, 1998.

The authors have modeled this book on Lavin's *Business Information: How to Find It, How to Use It* 3d ed. (Oryx, 2002). The work provides a handpicked selection of sources and is aimed at a novice audience.

Sheehy, Carolyn A., ed. *Managing Business Collections in Libraries*. Westport, Conn. and London: Greenwood, 1996.

Sheehy provides advice to selectors on how to improve their knowledge of business literature and plenty of recommended readings.

Slavens, Thomas P. *Using the Financial and Business literature*. New York: Dekker, 2004.

This book is divided into a section on electronic sources and a section on print sources of business information. The electronic sources include Web sites, online publications, and databases, and are presented as an

Ato Z annotated guide to sources on everything from accounting to zip codes. Although it contains almost exclusively reference material, the print sources section is organized by Library of Congress Classification, which is useful for comparing against your own library collection. The annotations are mainly descriptive and often do not evaluate the merit of the sources.

Wasserman, Paul, and Gale Research Company. *Encyclopedia of Business Information Sources.* Detroit: Gale Research 2004.

Encyclopedia is an apt description of this extremely comprehensive work that arranges entries by topic, then format, and finally publication title.

Weaver, Maggie. *The Canadian B2B Research Sourcebook: Your Essential Guide.* Toronto: Canadian Library Association, 2001.

Billed as "a quick start guide to market research," this book lists free and fee-based Internet sources. Entries are arranged by the North American Industry Classification System (NAICS) code. The book is unique because it focuses exclusively on Canadian business information.

White, Gary W. *The Core Business Web: A Guide to Key Information Resources.* New York: Haworth, 2003.

The Internet is by nature unstable, and although some of the Web sites in this book may no longer exist, many will endure, and the criteria provided for evaluating sites are still valuable.

Zagorsky, Jay L. *Business Information: Finding and Using Data in the Digital Age.* Boston and Toronto: McGraw-Hill, 2003.

This is a useful introduction to the variety of demographic, industry, and economic data and information that business users need. Even if some of the sources described in this book are already extinct, new business librarians will appreciate the clear explanations of the general categories of business information. Most chapters in this book include a section on Canadian and international information as well.

REVIEW ARTICLES

Peruse business and library literature for reviews of databases and lists of key resources on special topics. The following articles are just some examples:

McGuigan, Glenn. "Invisible Business Information: The Selection of Invisible Web Sites in Constructing Subject Pages for Business." *Collection Building* 22, no. 2 (2003): 68–74.

Meredith, Meri. "Developing an International Business Reference Collection." *Collection Management* 26, no. 4 (2001): 73–88.

Schnedeker, Donald. "Business and Economic Databases Access in Academic Business

Libraries." *Journal of Business and Finance Librarianship* 9, no. 1 (2003): 37–47.

Schwartz, Bill N., and Michelle C. Russo. "Auditing Accounting Databases." *Online* 26, no. 1 (Jan.–Feb., 2002): 36–43.

CORE JOURNALS

There are thousands of scholarly, popular, and trade business periodicals on the market. Because periodicals require an annual subscription cost and the ongoing maintenance of binding or Web site updating, these resources constitute a more serious investment than individual monographs. If you are in an academic library, take note of where your researchers are publishing. If you have access to Journal Citation Reports, you can get a list of the most highly cited journals in business, economics, and management. The Web site DOAJ: Directory of Open Access Journals hosts peer-reviewed business and economics journals available free of charge. Ulrich's International Periodicals Directory is a standard tool for periodicals information. Entries include the start year of the publication, price, frequency, format, where the periodical is indexed, and a brief review of the content and audience level. Ulrich's Serials Analysis System is a product that automatically compares a library's serials holdings against Ulrich's own list of core journals and identifies the gaps. Magazines for Libraries is another reference tool for determining core serials in a particular discipline. Each entry describes the serial and provides information about publication history, price, audience, and indexing. *The Serials Librarian* and *Serials Review* are quarterly journals covering issues in serials selection, acquisition, and access.

PUBLISHERS' CATALOGS AND WEB SITES

Publishers' catalogs can be picked up at conference trade shows or viewed online on publishers' Web sites. Many publishers' Web sites offer e-mail notification when new books are published in the areas in which you collect. Publishers' catalogs and Web sites are a good place to look for new books when you need to quickly spend a budget. This pleasant but somewhat alarming situation can happen near the end of a fiscal year or if you receive a monetary donation that must be spent immediately.

With time, you will become familiar with the publishers that best serve the needs of your user community. Earl Lee of Pittsburg State University, Kansas, writes, "One thing that a collection development librarian should learn fairly quickly is how to judge various publishers by what they produce. There are some publishers who can be relied on to produce a good book, day in and day out, because they have a commitment to producing literature that is clearly and cogently written . . . "[2]

The following publishers produce business or economics titles.

University Presses

The following university presses have a strong collection of business titles. The treatment tends to be more academic than popular, so expect to find a more research-oriented approach with lengthier lists of references.

Cambridge University Press
Columbia University Press
Cornell University Press
Duke University Press
Harvard Business School
Harvard University Press
McGill-Queen's University Press
University of Michigan
MIT Press
State University of New York Press
Oxford University Press
Princeton University Press
Stanford University Press
University of Chicago Press
University of Miami Press
University of Pennsylvania Press
University Press of America
University of Toronto Press
Wharton School Publishing
Yale University Press

Trade Presses

Several trade presses have developed rich catalogs of business monographs. Close inspection of a sampling of titles should give you a feel for how well the press meets your users' needs. In some cases, specific series of publications from a particular press may be valuable, while most of that press's other publications are not worth collecting. Some of these publishers make publications available as electronic books as well.

Allen and Unwin

> Australian publisher of popular books covers small business, management, human resources, sales and marketing, business communications, finance, accounting, economics, and industrial relations.

Ashgate Publishing

> Academic and professional publisher producing economics and business and management titles.

Barron's Educational Series

> Test preparation manuals, a line of business books, specialized dictionaries, handbooks, and guides.

Blackwell Publishing

> British publisher of scholarly books on accounting and taxation, banking and finance, business and management, and economics.

CABI Publishing

> Academic titles in leisure, recreation and tourism, and agricultural economics.

Crown Business

> An imprint of the Crown Publishing Group, books on management, leadership, and personal finance.

Edward Elgar

> Academic publisher of books on economics, finance, business, management, and law.

Elsevier

> A large global publisher of scholarly books, journals, and databases, covering business, management, accounting, decisions sciences, economics and finance.

Greenwood Press

Popular and professional titles covering the gamut of business and economics.

Haworth

Publisher of scholarly professional books.

Kogan Page

Primarily a business publisher of popular titles.

McGraw-Hill Ryerson

Textbooks and professional titles in all areas of business.

M. E. Sharpe

Reference books, textbooks, and general-interest books covering business, management, economics, marketing, finance, and banking.

Palgrave MacMillan

Academic and professional titles in the areas of business and economics.

Pfeiffer

Training books for human resources professionals.

Praeger Publishers

A division of Greenwood Publishing Group that publishes academic and general-interest titles on business and economics.

Prentice-Hall

Educational publisher of academic books and textbooks.

Rowman and Littlefield Publishers

Academic titles in business and economics.

Routledge

Academic works and textbooks on business and economics.

Sage Publications

Academic and professional business, management, and economics titles.

Saint Martin's Press

Popular titles in business.

Springer Science and Business Media

Academic titles in business and management and economics. Kluwer Academic is now part of Springer Science and Business Media.

Thomson Gale

Business reference books.

Wiley

Prolific publisher of titles on every business topic; the Jossey Bass imprint targets practitioners in business and management.

Association and Society Presses

AMACOM

Publishing division of the American Management Association.

American Institute of Certified Public Accountants

Publishes books on all aspects of tax and accounting.

Canadian Marketing Association

Publishes guides and handbooks on marketing-related topics in Canada.

Research Centers and Nongovernmental Organization Publishers

American Enterprise Institute for Public Policy Research

A strong proponent of small government and national defense, a Washington- based think tank publishing economics and politics titles.

Brookings Institution

Washington-based think tank on public policy, business, and economics.

Canadian Center for Policy Alternatives

Nonpartisan Canadian research institute investigating issues of economics and social justice.

C. D. Howe Institute

Nonpartisan Canadian public policy research institute based in Toronto, Ontario.

Colombia International Affairs Online

Publishes working papers and other research from a variety of research institutes, think tanks and nongovernmental organizations (NGOs) on international affairs.

Conference Board

New York–based nonprofit organization disseminating research about corporation management and the marketplace.

Conference Board of Canada

Nonprofit Canadian organization specializing in economic trends, organizational performance, and public policy.

Institute for International Economics

Washington-based nonpartisan, nonprofit research institute specializing in the study of international economic policy.

National Bureau of Economic Research

Nonprofit, nonpartisan research institute devoted to economic research for policymakers, business professionals, and academics.

RAND Corporation

With origins in the military industry, RAND (a contraction of "research and development") is a nonprofit organization dedicated to research in social, economic, and political issues.

World Bank

Dedicated to financial and technical aid for developing countries. Publication available by subscription to the e-Library

NOTES

1. OCLC, "2004 Information Format Trends: Content, Not Containers," OCLC Web site. Accessed Dec. 29, 2005, www.oclc.org/reports/2004format.htm.
2. Earl Lee, *Libraries in the Age of Mediocrity* (Jefferson, N.C.: McFarland, 1998), 54.

four

The Special Case of Online Databases

A business collection includes many types of materials: periodicals, mono-graphs, dictionaries and encyclopedias, directories, and online databases. Each type of material requires a thoughtful approach to selection, but it is online databases that can be the most daunting to a new selector because of the financial investment, licensing issues, and sheer complexity of the data-bases. With so much business information available for free on the Internet, the selector has to weigh the added value of the databases against the costs of the subscription. This is a critical issue because users can be quite adept at finding some of the business information they need for free on the Internet. They will only use expensive online databases if the databases are easy to navigate, provide information not available elsewhere, or have additional ma-nipulation or downloading features. Many business databases are designed with corporate library subscribers in mind and priced for the corporate—not academic or public library market. All of these factors complicate the selection work for the business librarian.

Some of the selection aids described in the previous chapter will aid in the selection of online databases. This chapter provides a checklist of criteria to consider as well as an overview of some of the major databases used at academic and public libraries on the market at the time of writing.

THE CHALLENGE

Databases are the most serious investment for any business collection. These resources normally demand a commitment to expensive annual subscription fees as well as a time investment to learn the databases' idiosyncrasies and to teach users how to effectively navigate them. If there were a core set of essential databases from which to select, these problems would be limited; however, the reality is that there are hundreds of databases on the market competing for your attention. Each of these databases presents its own interface, pricing model, scope of content, and functionality—all important factors that must be considered.

There are several other complications that make selecting databases a challenge. Many databases directly compete with one another by offering similar content. Some databases offer identical content with different search interfaces. Aggregators are databases that buy content from third parties, repackage it, and sell it to libraries. The aggregator does not usually own the content, but licenses it from the content creators, so the content of the databases is somewhat unstable and is added or deleted as licenses with creators are extended or expire. For example, EBSCO's Business Source Premier currently contains company profiles provided by Datamonitor and country reports by Business Monitor International and CountryWatch. Your library may subscribe to Datamonitor, Business Monitor International, or Country-Watch as separate databases and run the risk of duplicating the content offered through Business Source Premier.

Many databases are divided into modules that can be separately purchased. Mergent Online, for example, offers modules for company data, annual reports, equity and bond information, and industry surveys. Many other databases are not available in discrete packages, so you will find some overlap and duplication of information across your databases. This is inevitable, and it is not a waste of resources because you are providing your users with choices and an opportunity to compare the accuracy of different sources.

Obviously, the content of the database is the first thing to consider, but it is by no means the only factor. Your library may have a selection policy in place especially for databases. If not, this chapter lays out several important criteria to consider. The bottom line will always be: is the database valuable to the library users (both in terms of content and usability) and can the library afford the annual subscription?

Before you do subscribe to a database, request a free trial so you can test the product and solicit feedback from patrons and other library staff. Ask the database vendor for the names of current subscribers and contact these libraries for their impressions of the product and their satisfaction with the vendor's customer support. Once you have made a decision and purchased a subscription, the selection process continues as you monitor its use and determine each year whether to resubscribe. You can learn more about the databases on the market by attending vendor exhibits at conferences or by periodically scanning the Web pages of other libraries. Vendors are always happy to meet with you and describe the range of products that they offer.

CRITERIA FOR SELECTION

Business librarians are strongly encouraged to apply clear and stringent criteria to the selection of new databases—in much the same way that librarians encourage patrons to carefully evaluate the information they find on the Internet. Some criteria to consider:

- coverage;
- functionality;
- customer service and support; and
- cost.

Coverage

The first question to consider is whether the database contains information that is valuable and relevant to your users. Do your users require information about the local market, or are their needs more international in scope? Check that the geographical coverage of the database is appropriate. More and more databases are offering information beyond the North American and Western European markets, and there is now greater coverage particularly of Asia and Latin America available.

Is the information provided at a level of detail appropriate to your users' needs? As a rule, more in-depth and detailed information is more expensive. General surveys of industries are more available and affordable than analyses of very specialized markets or particular brands or products. Some faculty actually discourage academic libraries from collecting in-depth analytical business reports as they want their students to do the analytical work themselves.

How often is content refreshed and updated? Some online databases are updated minute by minute, while others are updated much less frequently or without a fixed schedule. Is information archived, and if so, for how long? Do new reports replace older ones, or can you continue to access older reports?

Once you have decided that a database provides the kind of information your users need, investigate the quality of that information. Is the source of the information and the manner in which it is collected clearly stated? The methods used to collect data and to generate research reports should be transparent. What are the credentials of the researchers and data collectors who create and collect the information in the database, and what are their biases in the presentation of information? Does the database contain primary data or secondary data derived from such sources as companies' annual reports? If you are considering a periodical database, is there an embargo period during which you can not access new periodical issues? Are periodical articles available in Portable Document Format (PDF), and do you get access to all of the periodical's content as you would with a print subscription, including advertisements, graphics, and classified ads?

Think about the database as a part of the whole collection. Does it overlap with other materials or fill significant gaps in your collection? Can you subscribe only to the most useful parts of the database instead of a full subscription? If you decide to purchase only a part, make sure the non-subscribed parts are not visible, as this is very frustrating to the user.

Functionality

There are many factors to consider when evaluating a database's functionality. Is it easy to search? Is there good online help? Can information be quickly and easily downloaded? Can you e-mail results to yourself or others? The greatest information is useless if it cannot be readily accessed. Most users are not professional searchers, and many will throw up their hands in frustration if an online database does not work almost as easily and instantaneously as Google. The old adage that "functionality is paramount" is typically used in relation to young users, but it might just as easily apply to all users.

The first database feature to test is the search function. Is the search field easy to find, and does a simple search produce at least some results? If too many searches return no results, users may become frustrated and give up — even if the data contained within is valuable. Does the search mechanism require precision, or does it try to match your input with the closest match in the database? Is there an advanced search function for better search control? Does the database provide a thesaurus or a browsing function? Is there context-relevant help, and are suggestions provided for modifying a search if no results are found?

Once users find the information they want, what can they do with it? A good database will provide several output options for data, such as Microsoft Excel or SPSS format, so that the user can manipulate the data once it has been exported. Users should be able to easily save, e-mail, print, or export information into a variety of bibliographic management programs.

You certainly will want to consider the capacity of the database server. Can you connect and download information quickly—even at peak times of the day? How often is the database server down for maintenance or because of capacity problems? Is there any issue with connecting to the database remotely through the library's proxy server? Is authentication to the database based on the library's IP addresses, or must users enter a username and password each time to login?

Is there any flexibility to customize parts of the database to suit the needs of your library, such as changing the default setting for the search page? Many databases can also provide some custom functions to individual users, such as saving searches and providing e-mail alerts when new information becomes available.

Customer Service and Support

Customer support is an important component of a database subscription, because there will inevitably be problems that need fixing or questions that need answering. Will the vendor promptly respond to your concerns and implement a solution? It is hard to know for sure in advance, but you can check with other libraries that already subscribe to the product to find out how responsive and supportive the vendor has been for them.

Business database vendors are expert users of the databases and may have a formal business education. Use their knowledge and expertise to help you do your job better. Most vendors provide training on their products, which may be available in the form of online tutorials or in-person or telephone training. In most cases, it is preferable to be trained by the vendor and to train your users yourself, rather than have the vendor directly train your users. You are most familiar with their needs and interests and can tailor a training session to users better than a vendor can. It also gives you another opportunity to meet your users face to face.

Vendors should provide you with usage statistics so you will know how often your users are accessing the database. This is very important information to take into account when it comes time to resubscribe.

Cost

Last but not least, you will have to consider the cost of the database. Databases rarely come with a set cost, but instead are priced according to a number of factors, including the number of potential users, whether your library subscribes to other products from the same vendor, and whether your library's subscription would be a feather in the vendor's cap. A large institution will pay more than a small one. The pay-per-use model which is used in some corporate libraries is not workable in most academic and public libraries, so in some cases, your library will pay for a certain number of *seats*, or the number of users who can access the database at one time. You should get reports from the vendor monitoring how often users are turned away because the maximum number of simultaneous users has been reached. This is a very frustrating situation for users who expect to be able to access databases whenever they need them.

Fortunately for the selector, the license agreement and the price are not usually negotiated by the selector but by an electronic services librarian or acquisition staff member with expertise in this area. In some cases, databases are negotiated as part of packages with other libraries in a consortium. Find out if a database can be purchased consortially (and thus more cheaply) before your library goes it alone.

SELECTED MAJOR ONLINE DATABASES

The online business databases most commonly found in public and academic research libraries in North America are described in this section. This is neither a comprehensive list, nor is it an endorsement of particular vendors. Highly specialized niche databases created solely for corporate and other special libraries are not included. Online directories have been omitted from this list, because they are self-explanatory and usually simply replacements of print editions. As a selector, you must decide which databases are the best fit for your library, based on your users' needs and your budget. Look for recent reviews and how similar databases stack up against each other in such periodicals as *Library Journal* and *The Information Advisor* (see chapter 3).[1]

The following databases are arranged according to the type of information they provide. If databases provide several different types of information, they are listed several times, although the database description is only given once. The publishing industry is in constant flux, so database names, content, and ownership may no longer be accurate. Check the database Web sites or contact the vendor for updates and clarification about products.

Accounting and Tax

In addition to the resources listed here, most of the databases listed in the Periodical and Full-text Databases section provide accounting and tax literature.

CCH Tax Research NetWork

CCH publishes tax and accounting books, journals, CD-ROMs, and online databases. The CCH Internet Tax Research NetWork provides U.S. federal and state tax information. The CCH Internet Research NetWork is a database of laws and regulations on federal securities, aviation, global securities, banking, telecommunications, energy, product liability, consumer safety, and information technology.

CICA Handbook

This CD-ROM covers Canadian accounting guidelines published by the Canadian Institute of Chartered Accountants.

Financial Accounting Research System (FARS)

FARS is a CD-ROM database of accounting literature produced by the Financial Accounting Standards Board.

ProQuest Accounting and Tax

See main entry in the Periodical and Full-text Databases section for a description.

Company Information

All company databases offer similar basic information on public companies: a brief description and history of the company, names of directors and executives, list of key competitors, and basic financial information from the company's public filings. Because much of this information can be found for free on company Web sites, it is the ease and sophistication of searching and exporting of information that add value to these subscription databases. Beyond these basics, some databases add more in-depth company profiles and histories, lists of subsidiaries and properties, several years' worth of financial information, ratios and spot data, investment guidance, and links to current news about the company. Some company databases provide better coverage than others and may include smaller companies, private corporations, and companies based outside of North America.

Bureau Van Dijk Electronic Publishing (BvDEP)

BvDEP publishes several business databases. Some of the databases most commonly found in academic libraries include AMADEUS, a database of European public and private companies; BANKSCOPE, a database of public and private banks; ORBIS, a database of 15 million global companies; and OSIRIS, a compendium of companies, banks, and insurance companies worldwide. Merger and acquisitions data is available on the ZEPHYR database. BvDEP also produces more than a dozen European country-specific company databases and is a provider of several Economist Intelligence Unit products.

Business Monitor Online

Produced by the British-based Business Monitor International, this is a truly international company, industry, news, and country information database. This resource covers the businesses and industries as well as political and economic risk analysis of 175 countries. Demographic data is also available.

Compustat

Standard and Poor's Compustat provides company data with up to twenty years of market history and five years of daily stock-price history. There are several different Compustat products, including Compustat North America, Compustat Global, and Compustat Historical. Market Insight, a component of Compustat is available as a subset and includes financial reports, executive compensation reports, and valuation ratios. Compustat products are available through the WRDS interface (see main entry the Finance section for a description).

Corporate Retriever

Micromedia ProQuest's Corporate Retriever is a database of Canadian public, private, and Crown corporations.

Dun and Bradstreet Million Dollar Database

This database provides financial and descriptive information about companies with more than $1 million in sales or more than twenty employees. The North American Million Dollar Database includes more than

1.5 million U.S. and Canadian public and private businesses, and information is updated monthly. The International Million Dollar Database has the same number of international companies.

EDGAR Online Pro

EDGAR (Electronic Data Gathering, Analysis, and Retrieval System) is a free online database of public company filings for the U.S. Securities and Exchange Commission. The EDGAR Online Pro version of the database provides enhanced searching and analyzing of company financial data.

Factiva

Factiva is a news and company information database in more than twenty languages. Some of the news sources are not available to academic library customers. Factiva is the only source for current access to one of Canada's national newspapers, *The Globe and Mail*. The company information includes contact information, business description, key competitors, key financials, charts, and related news.

FinancialPost Infomart

CanWest Global's FinancialPost Infomart is a Canadian public company, business news investment, and biography database. Two unique features are the Directory of Directors, a biographical directory of Canadian company directors, and Predecessor and Defunct, which provides name changes, acquisitions, and takeovers since 1929.

Hoover's Pro

Hoover's is available in different versions, from a stripped-down Hoover's Lite to the most robust Pro Premium. Hoover's Pro is targeted at academic libraries and lets the user build lists of companies based on selected criteria.

ISI Emerging Markets

See main entry in the Industry and Market Research section for a description.

LexisNexis Academic

Lexis began providing full-text legal information in 1973. Nexis started as a business information service six years later. Today, LexisNexis Group provides company data, market research, industry, news, legal publications, country reports, patent details, and a myriad of business reference tools, including company directories and biographical information. LexisNexis Academic (Canada) provides additional Canadian legal and news content.

MarketLine

MarketLine is a British-based database of company, industry, and country information. The company file contains approximately 10,000 businesses. In addition to basic company descriptions and financials, profiles include companies' products and main competitors, biographical details of executives and directors and SWOT analyses (a review of the companies' strengths, weaknesses, opportunities, and threats). Industry profiles are approximately twenty pages in length; they are based on interviews, surveys, and secondary research. Each industry profile contains five-year historical and five-year forecast of market values and volumes, market segmentations, major trends, leading companies, and a broad view of the market's competitive landscape strength. Country reports include demographic and macroeconomic data and commentary on each country's business and political climate.

Mergent Online

Mergent Online offers up to fifteen years of company financial data, annual reports, equity and corporate bond portraits, and industry reports for North America, Asia Pacific, and Europe in separate modules that can be purchased individually or in packages.

OneSource

OneSource is a database of public and private companies, business and trade periodical articles, analyst reports, and executive profiles, and it is available in five different editions emphasizing business information from different parts of the world: United States and Canada, United Kingdom, Europe, Asia Pacific, and Global.

Research for Libraries

Research for Libraries is a gateway to several databases including, among others, the company and industry database MarketLine (see previous description); the industry report database Business Insights (see main entry in the Industry and Market Research section for a description); ProductScan, a database of consumer packaged goods; and AccessAsia, which provides market commentary, executive profiles, and company profiles of businesses in Asia.

Standard and Poor's Net Advantage

This database has private and public company directories, public company financials, mutual fund reports, U.S. industry surveys, stock market analyses and stock recommendations, a directory of security dealers in North America, and a biographical directory of directors and executives. An added feature, the Learning Center, has a useful glossary of financial terms and short essays on investment advice.

Thomson Financial

See descriptions of Thomson Financial databases in the Finance section.

Thomson Gale's Business and Company Resource Center

This database provides quite comprehensive company profiles, including ownership relationships, products and brands, corporate histories, financials, and links to news and analysis. The larger Business and Company Resource Center—All Modules includes Investext Plus (see main entry in the Industry and Market Research section for a description), PROMPT (see main entry in the Periodical and Full-text Databases section for a description), and Newsletters ASAP (see main entry in the Periodical and Full-text Databases section for a description).

Country Reports

Country reports examine the risk and requirements of doing business in various countries based on a variety of economic, political, legal, and social conditions. Reports may include a risk rating, related news, forecasts, overview of the government and economy, tax laws and business regulations, and macroeconomic data.

Business Monitor Online

See main entry in the Company Information section for a description.

CountryData.com

The PRS Group publishes this database, which includes economic indicators and risk ratings for more than 140 countries.

CountryWatch

This database includes several modules: CountryReviews are periodically updated reports on the demographic, economic, political, business and cultural aspects of countries. CountryWire is a global newsfeed. CountryWatch Forecast is a five-year macroeconomic forecast for countries covered. CountryWatch Data and CountryWatch Map Gallery let the user select variables (for example, country, tourist arrivals, greenhouse gas emissions, mortality rate, etc.) to create comparison tables or maps.

Economist Intelligence Unit (EIU)

The Economist Intelligence Unit is suite of databases covering data and analysis about the economic, political, and business affairs of countries around the world. Content is provided through almost two dozen different data and information products, some updated daily, and others focusing on long-term economic indicators and forecasts. EIU is particularly useful for tracking operating conditions, commercial laws, and business regulations in countries. The products the selector will choose from the suite will depend on the particular needs and interests of the library's particular users.

Global Insight

Global Insight, formerly known as World Markets Research Centre, provides country reports covering country risk and forecasts, general business conditions, and the political, economic, regulatory, and tax environment. It is available through WRDS (see main entry in the Finance section for a description).

MarketLine

See main entry in the Company Information section for a description.

SourceOECD

SourceOECD is the Organization for Economic Cooperation and Development's online library of statistics, books, and periodicals.

Data and Statistics

These databases primarily contain data and statistics rather than textual information. Statistics of interest to business researchers include demographic and market-share data, business ratios, and all manner of data related to the economy, such as exchange rates, interest rates, and import and export data. Most business and economic statistics are collected by governments, research firms, and trade associations.

Business Monitor Online

See main entry in the Company Information section for a description.

Dun and Bradstreet Industry Norms and Key Business Ratios

Dun and Bradstreet provides fourteen business ratios arranged by Standard Industrial Classification Codes. Ratios are used to benchmark company performance against an industry as a whole.

CANSIM

CANSIM is Statistics Canada's database for socioeconomic data, with more than 18 million time series on a variety of topics, such as trade, investment, income, and labor.

EIU DataServices

See main entry in the Country Reports section for a description.

Inter-University Consortium for Political and Social Research (ICPSR)

ICPSR provides access to an archive of social science data, including census information, economic behavior and attitudes, and social indicators.

International Financial Statistics Online Service (IFS)

The IFS is the International Monetary Fund's database of 32,000 time series, such as exchange rates, commodity prices, and interest rates.

International Statistical Yearbook

This database is a compilation of key statistics from major organizations that collect economic statistics, such as the Organisation for Economic Co-operation and Development (OECD), the International Monetary Fund (IMF), and the European Union Statistical Office.

ISI Emerging Markets

See main entry in the Industry and Market Research section for a description.

LexisNexis Statistical

This database provides access to statistics produced by U.S. federal and state governments and agencies, international intergovernmental organizations, independent research organizations, and universities, and as such, it covers much more than economic and business statistics.

SourceOECD

See main entry in the Country Reports section for a description.

STAT-USA/Internet

The U.S. Department of Commerce's STAT-USA/Internet provides access to official business, trade and economic information. The site consists of two main databases: State of the Union (SOTN), a repository of U.S. economic indicators; and Global Business Opportunities (GLOBUS) and the National Trade Data Bank (NTDB), data for exporters.

TableBase

See main entry in the Periodical and Full-text Databases section for a description.

UN Comtrade Database

Limited access to United Nations commodity trade statistics is available for free on the Web. A subscription allows the user to download data, save queries, and create notification alerts.

World Bank

The World Bank produces books, documents and reports that may be accessed from the World Bank e-Library. World Bank's premier product, World Development Indicators is an online database of world economic and development data.

Finance

This category includes mostly data and some textual information on stocks, money, banking, bonds, mutual funds, and futures and options.

Bloomberg Financial Markets

Bloomberg provides real-time financial data—stock market indexes, equities, bonds, mutual funds, currencies, commodities, and futures—as well as historical pricing data, news, and company descriptions.

Center for Research in Security Prices (CRSP)

The University of Chicago's CRSP produces several time series databases. The CRSP US Stock Database provides historical daily stock market prices since 1925. CRSP has also teamed up with Standard and Poor's Compustat (see main entry in the Company Information section for a desscription) to offer the CRSP/Compustat Merged Database, which links CRSP stock data and Compustat fundamental data.

DBRS (Dominion Bond Rating Service)

DBRS is a privately owned Canadian rating agency that provides credit ratings and industry analysis.

Economática

This tool helps analyze equities and find company, stock, commodity, currency, and inflation data for selected South American countries.

Financial Performance Indicators

This Statistics Canada product contains key financial ratios and balance sheets for Canadian industries.

Morningstar.com Library Edition

This investment research database provides stock screening tools, financial data for 8,000 stocks and 13,000 funds, and analyst reports to guide investment decisions for the researcher or individual investor.

Standard and Poor's Net Advantage

See main entry in the Company Information section for a description.

Thomson Financial

The Thomson corporation publishes in the areas of law, education, science, healthcare, and finance. Thomson Financial division sells several major databases. Its flagship databases and those most often found in academic libraries are described here. Datastream Advance is a time series database of financial instruments, securities, and indicators. Data sets include equities, fundamentals, unit and investment trusts, indices, bonds, international macroeconomics, commodities, and interest and exchange rates. Investext Plus is a full-text database of investment research reports from investment banks and consulting firms, and it is useful for following industry trends, forecasts, and market share projections for publicly traded companies. Investext is available through LexisNexis. Thomson ONE is an investment management database comprised of several subdatabases (Baseline, StreetEvents, and PORTIA). Worldscope has current and historical information on companies worldwide. I/B/E/S History provides historical company data. VentureXpert is a database of venture funds. Thomson Research is a source for company information and analyst research reports. Thomson First Call links to institutional investors and brokerage firms for stock analyses and earnings estimates. SDC Platinum records financial transactions information.

Value Line Research Center

This database includes access to a number of Value Line investment publications, including its most well-known, the *Value Line Investment Survey*, providing weekly investment guidance. Data on equities, mutual funds, options, and convertibles can downloaded into graphs and tables.

Wharton Research Data Service (WRDS)

WRDS, developed by the Wharton School of Business at the University of Pennsylvania, is a Web interface for accessing a number of major business databases, including CRSP, Compustat, and Global Insight. The advantage WRDS provides is the capacity to search multiple financial, economic, accounting, marketing, and banking datasets with a common interface and consistent data output formats.

Industry and Market Research

Industry reports vary in length and content, but generally analyze the current environment and forecasted growth of a particular industry sector. Industry reports analyze the condition of an industry as a whole in a particular market, such as the automotive industry in the United States or the alcoholic beverages industry in Spain. They may include export and import data, taxation and regulation issues, key market players, and an outlook for the industry in the years to come.

Market research reports usually provide market segmentation, the major businesses competing in the market and their market share, pertinent macroeconomic and demographic data, trends, and forecasts. Individual reports are usually very costly, ranging from hundreds to thousands of dollars. Your users may request that you purchase them for your library, but the price and the narrow potential use of a single report usually makes this impossible. The market research reports in the databases listed here are more affordable because they are slightly out of date and are purchased as a package, but these reports still contain valuable information. Investigate the research methods used to collect the data in the reports, the level of detail, and whether it is primary research undertaken by a market research company for a client, or a compilation of several reports prepared by a third party. For further reading about market research, see:

Diamond, Wendy, and Michael R. Oppenheim. *Marketing Information: A Strategic Guide for Business and Finance Libraries.* Binghamton, N.Y.: Haworth, 2004.

James, Sylvia. "Compiling Global Market Research—A Tried and True Approach." *Business Information Alert* 15, no. 4 (May 2003): 1–4, 10.

Business Insights

This is a database of international market research reports for consumer goods, energy, financial services, healthcare, and technology.

Business Monitor Online

See main entry in the Company Information section for a description.

eMarketer

Reports cover e-business, online marketing, and emerging technologies and offer original market analysis combined with aggregated research from leading sources worldwide. eMarketer includes the EStat Database, a compilation of e-business statistics, charts, and articles.

Forrester Research

Forrester Research is a market research database with reports focusing on IT industries.

Frost and Sullivan

Frost and Sullivan is a market consulting firm that provides industry and market research reports on a range of industries. Market reports include market statistics, forecasts, and trends. Many libraries with a subscription do not provide access to all Frost and Sullivan reports, and some provide only mediated access.

Gartner intraWeb

This database covers market research reports on information techonology industries.

Global Market Information Database (GMID)

GMID is a product of Euromonitor International created especially for academic use. It is available in modules of market research reports and statistics. The reports cover 350 markets in more than 200 countries. Statistics are available on consumer markets, economic indicators, leisure and lifestyles, demographics, and much more.

IBISWorld

IBISWorld produces thirty-page industry reports that are updated every four months and detail key industry statistics and conditions, market characteristics and segmentation, key competitors, and forecasts.

InfoTech Trends

InfoTech Trends provides market research, statistics, and abstracts of industry journals on all areas of the information technology industry.

ISI Emerging Markets

ISI's flagship product is Emerging Market Information Service, an aggregate of market information, industry analyses, economic data, equity quotes, and news on emerging markets.' Other products include CEIC Data, for macroeconomic, industrial, and financial time series data from Asia; and The Islamic Finance Information Service (IFIS), for company profiles, news, and research reports in the Islamic financial world.

LexisNexis Academic

See main entry in the Company Information section for a description.

MarketResearch.com Academic

This is a collection of market research reports from approximately 350 market research firms covering a huge array of markets—from diapers to insurance companies. Special demographic reports are also available, such as the U.S. Multicultural Women Market and the Teens Market.

Mergent Online

See main entry in the Company Information section for a description.

Mintel Research Reports

Reports provide market forecasts and analyze industry trends in the European and U.S. markets. Reports range from retail to travel to the impact of flavors on the global food market.

Plunkett Research Online

Plunkett Research Online covers twenty-six industries with industry analysis, market trends, product overviews, and company information.

Snapshots International

As the name suggests, this database provides snapshots of international markets—coffee in Spain, hotels in France, game software in the United States, and so on. Snapshots reports are available as a pay-as-you-go option or as a regional package (more practical for a public library). The regional packages available are for the United Kingdom, Western Europe, Eastern Europe, Scandinavia, North America, Latin America, and Asia Pacific.

Sports Business Research Network (SBRNet)

SBRNet provides market research and industry news on the sporting goods and sports marketing industry.

Standard and Poor's Net Advantage

For a full description of Standard and Poor's industry surveys, see main entry in the Company Information section.

Thomson Finance

See main entry in the Finance section for a description.

Patents and Trademarks

Patent searching can be done directly in a patent depository library like the United States Patent and Trademark Office (www.uspto.gov) or through a third-party patent database, such as the following databases.

Derwent Innovations Index

Thomson Scientific's patent index includes patent records from Derwent World Patents Index and Patents Citation Index.

LexisNexis Academic

See main entry in the Company Information section for a description.

PatentWeb

This is MicroPatent's full-text and image database of U.S. and European patents.

Periodical and Full-text Databases

These databases are mainly aggregators of content from newspapers, journals, and industry and trade publications covering a broad spectrum of topics in business and economics. Some of these text databases offer working papers, monographs, reports, and government policy papers as well. Unfortunately, although the business librarian can choose a database, the specific selection of periodicals in an aggregated database is beyond the selector's control, as Bodi and Maier-O'Shea point out: "We have no control over all of the journals included in a database for which we are paying: we subscribe to a database for 10 journals in particular and pay for another 50 we do not need. We no longer have a physical collection over which we control what we purchase. . . ."[2]

Canadian Business and Current Affairs Business (CBCA)

ProQuest Micromedia's CBCA Business indexes articles published in Canadian business publications.

Columbia International Affairs Online (CIAO)

CIAO was created by Columbia University libraries and the Columbia University Press as a repository of economics and political science working papers, journals, books, policy briefs, and case studies on international affairs.

Conference Board and Conference Board of Canada

These full-text databases cover economic and business management reports that fall under the categories of leadership, human resources, corporate governance, regional, national, and international economic analyses, and more.

EBSCO Periodical and Full-text Databases

EBSCO's Business Source Premier and Business Source Complete compete with ProQuest's ABI/INFORM Global (see next page) for the academic library market. Theses resources include several thousand periodicals plus country economic reports, industry reports, yearbooks, and market research reports. Business Source Complete is a newer and more comprehensive version of Business Source Premier. As with ABI/INFORM Global, it broadly covers business with periodicals from the fields of economics, management, accounting, marketing, human resources, and so on. Business Source Elite is a smaller version of the Premier database and is aimed at smaller colleges and public libraries.

EconLit

EconLit, published by the American Economic Association, indexes the full spectrum of literature on economics back to 1969. The journals, working papers, dissertations, and journals indexed here are truly international in scope, and all subdisciplines of economics are covered—from agricultural to urban economics.

Elsevier Integrated Solutions in Business, Management and Economics

A giant science, technology, medicine, and social sciences publisher, Elsevier offers its business journals, online book series, and online business and economics reference works through its ScienceDirect and Scopus databases.

Emerald Management Xtra

Emerald is a publisher of management and library science journals. This database brings together Emerald's management journal collection and abstracts from another 300 top management journals, such as *Harvard Business Review* and *Sloan Management Review*. Other features of the database include collections of case studies, interviews with leading business figures, literature reviews, and book reviews.

Factiva

See main entry in the Company Information section for a description.

EBSCO Hospitality and Tourism Index

EBSCO's Hospitality and Tourism Index indexes and abstracts scholarly literature and industry news from the hospitality and tourism industries.

JSTOR

JSTOR is a nonprofit organization that produces full-text back issues of scholarly journals. The Business Collection includes more than forty titles in economics and finance drawn from the Arts and Sciences I, II, and IV packages.

LexisNexis Academic

See main entry in the Company Information section for a description.

Management and Organization Studies

This full-text database covers journals published by SAGE in the fields of business, management, and economics, 1971–present.

National Bureau of Economic Research (NBER) Working Papers

NBER, a U.S. nonprofit research center, offers subscription access to its working papers.

InfoSci-Online

This full-text database provides access to literature on trends, technologies, and challenges in the fields of information science, e-commerce, multimedia, and business management.

ProQuest Periodical and Full-text Databases

Proquest offers several periodical full-text, index, and abstract databases. ABI/INFORM Global is the largest with more than 1,000 scholarly and trade publications indexed. ABI/INFORM Trade and Industry indexes

periodicals and newsletters with a focus on trade and industry. ABI/
INFORM Research and ABI/INFORM Select are smaller versions of
ABI/INFORM Global, and are intended for public libraries and undergraduate research libraries. ABI/INFORM Dateline covers regional
business publications and newswires. ProQuest European Business,
ProQuest Asian Business, ProQuest Accounting and Tax and ProQuest
Banking Information Source are self-explanatory in the types of publications they cover. The ProQuest databases are aggregating databases that
include some nonperiodical types of information such as Hoover's company profiles, Going Global Career Guides, and EIU ViewsWire.

Social Science Research Network (SSRN)

SSRN and partner networks Accounting Research Network, Economics Research Network, Financial Economics Network, and Management
Research Network aim to make social science research available quickly
through the dissemination of abstracts of new publications and the pro-
motion of interchange between scholars in the same field.

SourceOECD

See main entry in the Country Reports section for a description.

Special Issues

Special Issues tracks and provides access to the content of special issues
published occasionally by business and trade magazines, such as product
overviews, industry outlooks, statistical information, salary surveys, and
company ranking lists.

Thomson Gale Periodical and Full-text Databases

Gale provides a number of periodical and full-text databases for business
researchers. Business and Company Profile ASAP is an index and full-
text database of business and economics journals with company directories. PROMT (Predicast's Overview of Markets and Technology) features
abstracts and full-text of trade from business journals and newspapers.
Newsletters ASAP is a full-text database of industry newsletters. Business
Dateline is a full-text database of about 350 regional business journals
and daily newspapers. Business Reference Suite is a suite of three databases: Business and Industry, Business and Management Practices, and
TableBase. Each is also available as a separate product. Business and
Industry includes more than 1,700 business journals, newspapers, and
trade publications from 1994 to today. Business and Management Prac-

tices is a relatively small database of approximately 300 professional and trade journals that emphasize the practical side of business and management. TableBase extracts tables from business periodicals and puts them in one place for quick access to data on companies, macroeconomics, market share, trends, and demographics.

Thomson Scientific's ISI Web of Knowledge

Thomson Scientific's ISI Web of Knowledge provides access to Social Science Citation Index, an index to publications in the social sciences, including business, management, and economics.

Wilson Business Abstracts and Full Text

These databases of academic and industry publications are of a similar breadth of subject covered, by EBSCO's Business Source Premier and ProQuest's ABI/INFORM Global [but with fewer publications].

NOTES

1. A recent review of online business databases appears in Gail M. Golderman and Bruce Connolly, "Briefcases and Databases: Web-based Reference Sources for Business Librarians and Their Client Communities," *The Reference Librarian* 44, no. 92 (2005): 235–61.
2. Sonia Bodi, and Katie Maier-O'Shea, "The Library of Babel: Making Sense of Collection Management in a Postmodern World," *The Journal of Academic Librarianship* 31, no. 2 (2005): 144.

five

Advice from a Seasoned Selector

THE BUSINESS COLLECTION is never *done*. Hundreds of new books are published each month. New topics emerge to baffle even the most seasoned librarian. The veteran selector still broods over new releases. The decisions between new packages and new formats get easier—but they never go away.

As the years pass, however, the new selector's comfort with the selection process tends to grow. The sheer mechanics of identifying promising titles and placing the orders (a Herculean task in some institutions!) becomes rote. Selectors slowly develop a clearer understanding of how the collection is used. They also become more familiar with the caliber and tone of material published by various houses. And in many cases, with time, the process of building or nurturing a good business collection becomes both an intellectual pursuit and a labor of love.

How can the new recruit accelerate the shift from crisis to confidence? The following areas warrant careful attention.

THE COLLECTION POLICY

If your organization does not have a formal collection policy, get to work writing one. The collection policy becomes your official statement of what you do and do not purchase. Such a document should be vetted with your user population and prominently featured on the library Web site. An effective statement also indicates the level at which you collect in that area. A well-honed statement reduces the number of questions at the selection stage. (For example, you don't need to think about purchasing a scholarly book on a specific topic if you're only committed to purchasing that topic at the general audience level.)

For assistance in creating an effective collection policy, take a look at some of the many excellent documents that libraries have posted on the Internet in recent years. Consider the collection policy, like the collection itself, as a dynamic entity that requires continuous stewardship. For academic libraries, conduct a systematic analysis of the collection policy against the most current version of the course calendar. For public libraries, compare the collection policy against the industrial sectors of your local community. Regardless of the library type, put your document forward for scrutiny. Ask for advice regarding new topics; be sure to purchase books at the most appropriate reading level for the intended readers of these books. And, at the same time, ask for advice regarding which topics should be downgraded or eliminated in your policy.

AVOID THE COMFORT ZONE

Less-seasoned selectors tend to buy heavily in areas they feel most comfortable with and neglect areas in which they are less versed. For example, the new recruit with a social sciences background may tend to beef up the human resources and marketing sections while ignoring the more technical finance and information systems titles. The slips keep getting pushed to the bottom of the pile in the hopes that insight will come. In a fit of desperation to order *something* in a particularly challenging field, the novice selector might rely to heavily on words in the title to determine relevancy. Over time, such tendencies create imbalances in the collections that may take years to undo.

The best strategy to avoid the comfort trap requires some honest reflection. Recognize where your gaps are and seek counsel from the experts. Academic librarians may ask the faculty from that area for assistance in identifying the best publishers, authors, and titles on an unfamiliar topic—at least while getting their feet wet on the job. Public librarians may seek advice from their network of contacts in the local community. You'll find that simply reviewing their choices will, over a short period of time, shed light on complex areas while still keeping the flow of new material onto the shelves.

THE NEW-BOOK SHELF

Careful examination of incoming material is one of the easiest but often neglected ways of building a strong collection. Consider locating new arrivals in a separate section—not just to facilitate use by patrons and showcase your hard work—but also as a convenient spot for you to review your choices. Take a good look at the level and comprehensiveness of the treatment, the quality of the binding, and so on. Academic libraries will also want to look at the depth of indexing and the extent of the footnotes and bibliographies. Did the book meet your expectations? Would you consider ordering other books from the same publisher or the same author? And if the book is a dud, make a note of the source to avoid future mistakes.

Then, depending on the setup of your library, monitor the level of buzz around the area. When titles fly off the new-book shelf, you have chosen well.

WEEDING

Weeding the collection is essential for effective user access and shelf management. The unweeded collection soon overflows its shelves and, like an untended garden, becomes underutilized and undervalued. Weeding is especially important in the reference area: a large, untamed collection scares off potential users and staff alike.

Novice selectors tend to underestimate the amount of time required for culling the shelves: the process is painstaking to do well. Circulation records or date stamps can be helpful for flagging possible withdrawals or transfers—but some intellectual work is required before a final decision can be made. The great classics may not be borrowed for home use, but these books are regularly consulted in the library. Consideration has to be given to library-wide policies regarding withdrawing earlier editions of the same book or copies held in multiple locations. In some cases, currency is paramount, and the user would be best served by withdrawing an older item and ordering a copy of the latest edition.

When possible, try to work weeding into your daily routine. When the new edition of a book is ordered, take the extra time to review the older versions. Examine holdings carefully when reviewing donations. Clean up as you go along rather than waiting for the special weeding project that never seems to get off the ground.

TALKING UP THE COLLECTION

Engaging users in frank discussions about the collection can be a frightening but ultimately rewarding experience. Collection analysis studies can identify obvious gaps in the collection, but only the users can place the results in the proper context. The expert selector wants to know where the weak areas are in relation to the users' actual needs. Tapping into this discussion takes some work: Consider holding focus groups with your user groups to see where work needs to be done. Seek input through your Web page. Academic librarians may wish to e-mail faculty for comments on the collection. Special librarians may ask for time on the agenda at departmental meetings.

HARVESTING BOOK RECOMMENDATIONS

Consider book recommendations as rich opportunities to test and strengthen your collection. If the recommended title meets your collection policy and appears to be of merit, how was it missed in the original selection process? Is there a publisher you should be watching out for in the future? Are there other books on the same topic that might actually be more current or more useful to the requestor?

THE LOCAL TOUCH

Standardized lists of best books may fail to capture local needs and areas of interest. To counteract this weakness, academic librarians may wish to consider reviewing their collections against faculty CV's. Do you own at least one copy of each tenured faculty member's key monographs? Make a point of learning what faculty members have published and the areas in which they do their research. The business librarian working in a corporate environment may wish to cull the company management directory in the same fashion. The public librarian should be watching for local company histories and business biographies — as well as books relating to key industries with a local presence.

SYSTEMATIC ANALYSIS

Once you have achieved some familiarity with your collection, consider testing it against recognized standards. Watch for lists of best books in specific subject areas. These carefully culled lists, frequently published in periodicals, help you identify the must-have titles in an unfamiliar field.

On a larger scale, consider comparing your collection against the University of Florida George A. Smather's Library's Business Books Core Collections (http://web.uflib.ufl.edu/cm/business/books/books.htm). This detailed listing of approximately 8,000 carefully selected books is divided into eighty discrete core fields.

PROMOTION

More seasoned selectors will want to more prominently showcase their great finds. Lists of new acquisitions, which can sometimes be automatically generated through your online catalog, would make popular links on your home page. Consider enriching your selections with book jacket visuals if your system will allow it. In-library displays can be laborious to maintain, but these displays are often very popular with users. Place your new-book shelf in a prominent place and position comfortable chairs around it to encourage lingering.

TEACHING

Use library instruction or information literacy sessions to educate users about the scope and breadth of the collection. Make use of classroom time to illustrate the added value associated with subscribed resources (versus free Internet sites) and to persuade dubious students of the benefits of mastering relatively convoluted library interfaces. Watch how your users interact with the online databases during hands-on sessions. Scrutinize the questions asked during sessions to identify areas where additional print or online content is required. Make the most of your discussions with faculty to identify new areas of emphasis and to sell your collection as a primary tool in the learning process.

Promote your collection to senior management relentlessly. Never assume that your dean or trustee recognizes the true value of expensive library resources. (Don't be alarmed when you hear even the most seemingly enlightened manager question the wisdom of a new or proposed product.) The proof is always in the pudding—in this case, the live demonstration or the testimonial.

EXPANDING LEARNING OPPORTUNITIES

The more-experienced selector will also want to begin broadening their professional development plan beyond standard library courses and conferences. Attendance at sessions geared toward practitioners, such as a GIS session for marketers or a hot-trends issue for human resources professionals, will hone your knowledge base and enhance your credibility with your user group.

FINAL THOUGHTS

Finally, new selectors are encouraged to enjoy the building process. Take pride in selecting that wonderful new encyclopedia set about which the reference librarians are all raving. Pat yourself on the back when an infrequent patron starts coming in regularly to check out the new titles. The learning curve is not insurmountable. The once-daunting task of selecting business materials may very well become the most rewarding aspect of your professional career.